# KINGDOM ON THE RHINE

History, Myth and Legend in Wagner's Ring

Nancy Benvenga

Anton Press
Harwich
1983

Dedicated to

Kammersänger KARL RIDDERBUSCH

Quotations from *The Nibelungenlied*, trans. A.T. Hatto, and *The History of the Franks*, trans. Lewis Thorpe, reprinted by permission of Penguin Books Ltd. Quotations from *I Saw the World End* by Deryck Cooke reprinted by permission of Oxford University Press.

Drawings are by Lars Feuk. The map on p. 24 is by the author.

ISBN 0 946380 00 7

Published by Anton Press, 27 Marine Parade, Dovercourt, Harwich, Essex.

Typeset and printed by Wm. Stevenson Printers, Ipswich, Suffolk.

# Table of Contents

# Foreword

In 1971 I decided that it was time for me, a long-time afficionado of French music, to come to terms with Wagner. My initiation took place through the gracious assistance of Mr. Edward Downes, who was then conducting the final showing of the Hotter production of the *Ring Cycle* at Covent Garden, and Mr. David Shaw, who arranged with Mr. Downes for me to be allowed to attend all the dress rehearsals of *The Ring,* which I did, armed with miniature orchestral scores.

The most memorable moment of that experience, for me at least, occurred when the curtain opened on Act I Scene 1 of *Götterdämmerung.* Two obviously royal personages were seated on thrones, but the stage was dominated by a third figure, a tall, dark man with intense, intelligent eyes. Who was he going to be? I wondered, and from then on I carefully followed his every action until the end.

My acquaintance with *The Ring* prior to this was of a most perfunctory nature, as I had only read the libretto once before (the scores that accompanied me to Mr. Downes' rehearsals were borrowed for the occasion) but no commentaries, interpretations or other such works; I was therefore without any prejudices as to which characters were the 'good guys' or the 'bad guys' respectively. Thus it was the mighty figure of Hagen as portrayed by the unsurpassable Karl Ridderbusch that had aroused my fascinated attention. Through Ridderbusch was revealed to me not Hagen's so-called 'villainy' but the heights of his commanding power as well as the depths of his turbulent emotions.

Obsessed with the desire to analyse the Hagen figure completely I bought my own score of *Götterdämmerung* which I could annotate to my heart's content, and immersed myself in the music. Then, in order to learn more about the origins of the characters, I read *The Nibelungenlied* in A.T. Hatto's absorbing translation. Not only did the mediaeval epic confirm my intuitive feelings that Hagen, far from being a mere cardboard villain, was in fact its most powerful figure, but Hatto's extensive and illuminating notes stimulated me to still further investigations, until eventually I found myself reaching beyond the legends as enshrined in the extant literature – the *Poetic Edda, Volsunga Saga* and *Thidrekssaga* as well as the *Nibelungenlied* – to the recorded historical events from which the literary works derived much of their inspiration. My odyssey into history then opened new horizons in making me realise that the origins of the Nibelung legend as a whole were just as intriguing as those of the Hagen figure. The result was this complete investigation of those actual events and personages which directly or indirectly, consciously or unconsciously, inspired or contributed to the vast body of literature, from the earliest primitive lays through the stark, simple Nordic poems through the expansive mediaeval epics, which ultimately formed the sources for the *Ring Cycle*.

In delving into history one finds the most fruitful period to be in and around the fifth century A.D., the time of the great Migrations, during which a Burgundian king named Gundahari – or Gunther – met his fearful destruction along with his entire kingdom, and the Hun leader Attila, the Scourge of God, struck terror into the hearts of all, barbarian tribesman and Roman citizen alike. But the centuries preceding and following this period are also not without importance, both the Roman Empire in its glory and the Merovingian dynasty of Frankish kings yielding a rich treasury of people and events that met their ultimate reincarnation in the brash and dazzling Siegfried, the weak, vacillating Gunther, the double-dealing but all-powerful and indispensable Hagen.

As the sub-title of the book implies, mythology is included in the discussion alongside history and legend. Indeed this is natural and inevitable, for myths and religion were *part* of the history of those peoples whose fate has passed into heroic legend and who have shaped those legends. Myth and history have interacted so closely in the formation of the legends that to ignore myth and concentrate exclusively on history – 'in a vacuum', as it were – would convey a seriously distorted impression of historical influence on Wagner.

In this connection it is important to explain my uses of the terms 'myth' and 'legend' and their related adjectives. To many people they are interchangeable, but I have chosen to draw a distinction between the two, a distinction which is rooted in the respective origins of the two phenomena. 'Legends' derive more closely and more directly from recorded history and are a form of enshrinement of ultimately actual heroes and events (and/or combinations thereof). 'Myths', on the other hand, represent man's attempt to come to terms with, explain and relate to phenomena he cannot readily and rationally understand; an obvious and convenient term would be 'God', but more specifically I am referring to aspects of the mechanics of nature for which no natural explanation was possible in terms of the science (or because of the lack of it) at the time. The resultant 'supernatural' explanation formed what we now call a myth; a good example is the attribution of the origin of earthquakes to the tremblings of Loki when snake venom dripped on his face as he lay bound to a rock in punishment for having caused the death of Balder. Obviously no such cut-and-dried distinction between Myth and Legend can apply universally, but as a general guideline in terms of this book it is a convenient one.

Further, some attention is given to the music only where relevant. This means that if the musical treatment seems uneven due to the music for some characters receiving more attention than that for others, it is because in no case is any musical analysis undertaken for its own sake, but only insofar as the music involved expresses or reflects qualities or concepts important in the context, whether historical, mythical or legendary.

Finally, I want to emphasise that this study of the historical precedents for the characters and events of the *Ring Cycle* does not propose to be another *interpretation* of the tetralogy: it does not promise the reader any profound new insights into the 'meaning' of Wagner's work. This would, at any rate, be impossible, by reason of the fact that the concentration on history will not allow for an equal look at all parts of *The Ring;* rather, the scrutinising spotlight will shine most strongly on *Götterdämmerung* and to a somewhat lesser extent on *Siegfried* and *Die Walküre*. The chief intention with this study is that an increased knowledge of the evolutionary process of certain aspects of *The Ring,* arrived at through a 'confrontation' between Wagner's characters and their ultimate historical models, may enrich the reader's enjoyment and appreciation of Wagner's greatest masterpiece.

For the sake of brevity I have used the following abbreviations in the text: VS – Volsunga Saga; NL Nibelungenlied; Ths. – Thidrekssaga.

With the exception of quotations from the NL, which are from Hatto's translation, and isolated instances of brief excerpts from Snorri's *Edda,* which are from Brian Branston's *Gods of the North* (the lengthy quote from Snorri in Chapter Five is my translation from Björn Collinder's Swedish version), all translations of quotations are my own. Material from the *Poetic Edda* I have translated from a combination of: *Edda, die Lieder des Codex Regius* (original language), *Den poetiska Eddan* (Swedish translation by Björn Collinder, from which I also translated the VS excerpts), *Die Edda* (German translation by Felix Genzmer) and *Valda sånger ur Eddan* (Swedish translation by Karl Ljungstedt). Wagner, of course, is translated from the original text.

The following 'score card' of the characters' names in the various sources may prove helpful:

| WAGNER | NL | | EDDA. VS | THS. |
|--------|-----|--|-----------|------|
| | Siegfried | | | Sigurd | |
| Brünnhilde | Brunhild | | | Brynhild | |
| | Hagen | | | Hogni | |
| | Gunther | | | Gunnar | |
| Gutrune | Kriemhild | | Gudrun | | Grimhild |
| Gibich | Dancrat | | Giuki | | Aldrian |

# 1

# The Literature:
# A General Survey

*Götterdämmerung* Act I begins with Gunther asking Hagen:

> Is my prestige on the Rhine
> worthy of Gibich's fame?

Well might the Rhenish king be concerned. In the period from which came Gunther's, Siegfried's and Hagen's historical predecessors intrigue, envy, instability and insecurity of political leaders were the order of the day. Indeed, not only the Germanic tribes of the Migration Period but even the Roman Empire and the Emperor himself were not immune; already in the first century A.D. Tacitus[1] records how the Emperor Domitian's jealousy of his own power and prestige brought about the destruction of Agricola, conqueror and governor of Britain, for Domitian could not suffer military glory to be snatched away from him and thus have a subject exalted above himself. This situation – envious and ineffectual emperors plotting against the military geniuses who were the true winners of glory for the Empire – repeats itself over and over in Roman history. In turn, discord among the numerous Barbarian tribes, not to mention between aspiring leaders within a tribe, was prevalent, and indeed was welcomed by the Romans; as Tacitus observed, 'Fortune can bestow on us no better gift than discord among our foes.'[2] Later, the Merovingian Period in Frankish history brought its own brand of political unruliness, fostered by the dictates of the inheritance law governing the rulers:

> . . . Fraternal wars and murders of relatives . . . were not
> uncommon. The confusion was promoted by the inheritance law
> of the Merovingians, whereby upon the death of the ruler the
> kingdom was divided among his sons . . . [who] therefore strove
> to attain sole rulership. [3]

Over the centuries events with such common elements as
fraternal strife, envy and betrayal merged in the minds of the
people to form patterns which in turn provided the framework
for the legends that developed into the great body of literature
now under our scrutiny. Thus in virtually no case can a
character or event in a poem or epic be traced directly back to a
single historical model: instead, several historical personages
or events with these common features would be combined into
one legendary one, the legend extracting 'from the lives of such
persons those occurrences and features that lend themselves to
the established picture of their heroes'.[4] Moreover, two events
originally unrelated and perhaps even many years apart would
sometimes be linked in a cause-and-effect relationship, for
example the later event being made into an act of retribution
for the earlier.

The very earliest Germanic poetry was associated with
religious services and cult worship. Already, in the Bronze Age
(1000–500 B.C.) symbolic acts and dances formed part of the
rites of the ancient Germans. These rites were accompanied by
the music of the lurs, which were curving, conical bronze horns
on the ends of which were discs decorated with embossed
ornaments. The length of the lurs, ranging from 1.5 to 2.3
metres, made them larger than most modern wind instruments,
and because of their soft and noble timbre they were suited for
use as cult instruments rather than for battle signals.[5] One of
their functions must have been to impart an air of solemnity to
the funerals of brave warriors, for even in ancient times such
rites were accompanied by solemn choruses commemorating
the heroic deeds of the dead man. Thus the trumpets which
ring out the Sword motif in Siegfried's Funeral Music in
*Götterdämmerung* are a modern echo of these ancient lurs

which performed a similar service for the Wagnerian hero's now long-forgotten 'ancestors'.

The Germanic tradition known as heroic poetry proper – the composing of poems or songs about events or persons that played an important role in the respective tribes' history – has its roots in the first century B.C., when the Goths, the greatest of the German tribes, left their Scandinavian home in search of new lands for their growing population. Crossing the Baltic Sea, they settled first in the area of the Weichsel River (roughly present-day Poland). It was the circumstances associated with this move – situations of adversity, such as the inevitable conflicts with the inhabitants of the new areas they sought to occupy, or the deeds of heroic leaders such as the legendary Filimer under whom the Goths first ventured forth from Scandinavia – that gave birth to Germanic heroic poetry. The memories of such adventures, which reached their culmination in the unsettled, stormy years encompassing the Migration Period of the fourth and fifth centuries, were enshrined in poems, lays and ballads which found their ultimate fruition in the great wealth of literature that formed the basis of Wagner's *Ring Cycle*.

The Roman historian Tacitus (*ca.* 55-120 A.D.) writes that the German tribes, even in the very early days of the Roman Empire, had a tradition of heroic song. In addition to describing the well-known chant called *baritus,* a type of war chant used to kindle the German tribesmen's courage when they rushed into battle, Tacitus informs us that the Germans sang the praises of 'Hercules', the foremost of all heroes, when they were going into battle.[6] The German equivalent of Hercules is the Teutonic god Donar, or Donner of *Das Rheingold.*

Of the very earliest lays, from before, during and immediately following the Migration Period, regrettably virtually nothing survives. There was no written tradition at this time; all poems were orally transmitted and subject to the alterations of each reciter, so that they survived unchanged in their essence but changeable in superficial details. It is evidence of the irrepressible vitality of this early poetry that, despite these circumstances as well as repression by the Church which was anxious to stamp out anything which harked back to paganism, the heroic legends survived in some form attractive enough to inspire subsequent poets until eventually the great literature was produced which survives today.

The primitive lays played a vitally significant role in early Germanic life because, in the absence of any written laws, through their enshrinement of the ancient values and virtues they incorporated the closest thing to an ethic code. For example, the two most highly-regarded virtues for the ancient Germans were honour and loyalty. In the honour of the individual lay that of his entire kin. One insulting word, any harm done to a relative, an offence against his right of possession required the German to avenge the insult at whatever risk to his life. Loyalty determined treaties, oaths and other mutual bargains entered into, whether, for example, between lords and knights or man and wife; this mutuality was an essential characteristic of loyalty, so that if the one party was suspected of being a traitor, the suspicious party was no longer bound. The linked themes of honour and loyalty must have recurred frequently in early heroic poetry, just as they do in the extant literature which evolved from it; for the avenging both of injured honour and of betrayal are central to the Nibelung legend.

At the height of the Migration Period and later, for example during the time of the Merovingian kings, the heroic poems and songs were performed by singers who accompanied themselves on a lyre. Such instruments are still preserved, one having been found in the grave of a Frankish singer in Cologne. They resembled the ancient Greek lyre, were made of wood and had six strings that could be tuned to different pitches. These singers, who might, for example, recite their lays as after-dinner entertainment at a prince's court, enjoyed quite an exalted position in society.

Many of the early lays must have described the general in terms of the particular, reducing important events involving entire nations to interactions between individuals:

> Not nations but personalities are the stuff from which the sagas are made: heroic deeds and the adventures of kings and knights are reported, while the names of the peoples are obscured in darkness . . . Not nations but rulers, families and the lord's retinues appear as allies and as enemies. [7]

An ancient Visigothic ballad, extant only in fragmentary form, recalls the Battle on the Catalaunian Plains in 541 A.D., in which the Huns and their allies suffered a major setback to their power at the hands of the other Barbarian nations united under the great Roman general Aëtius, by depicting the battle in terms of the strife between two Gothic brothers, one of whom fought on the side of the Huns and the other against them.[8] This Germanic tradition of hostile brothers, one of whom usually kills the other, has survived in *The Ring* in the case of Alberich and Mime, but, even more significantly for our study, in the relationship between Hagen and Gunther.

For the earliest surviving literature to incorporate the Nibelung legend and thus provide source material for *The Ring* one must look farther North, to Iceland, to the collection of poems dealing with the old Teutonic gods and heroes, known as the *Poetic Edda* to distinguish it from Snorri Sturlusson's *Prose Edda,* a handbook on mythology. In 1643 the Icelandic bishop Brynjólfur Sveinsson became the owner of an old manuscript anthology of poems on the old gods and heroes, which he erroneously interpreted as the work of his compatriot Saemundr Fródi (1056-1133); hence the collection has sometimes been known as *Saemund's Edda.* Today this manuscript is housed in the Copenhagen Royal Library under the name Codex Regius.

Exactly when the poems of the *Edda* were composed is not certain; they were probably created over a long stretch of time, from 800 to 1300, and many of the older ones existed a long while in oral tradition before being committed to parchment, for the written tradition did not exist before 1220. Researches estimate the Codex Regius manuscript to date from the end of the thirteenth century. The style differs from poem to poem; the stark archaism of some points to their stemming directly from an oral tradition, while others seem to have been written by educated men.

The *Edda* is divided into poems about the gods and poems about the heroes; it is chiefly the latter which will concern us. In the Codex Regius they are arranged in the approximate chronological order of the events described, although this internal chronology does not in the least coincide with the order in which the poems were composed. Prose additions fill in occasional gaps in the action arising from such factors as the absence of some pages of the poetry text. The poems chiefly revolve around the life of Sigurd Fafnersbane (Siegfried in *The Ring*), his heroic deeds, his death and the subsequent events involving his kin. The first few poems describe the lives of Sigurd's Volsung ancestors, Sigurd's early years, including the story of his foster-father Regin the dwarf (Wagner's Mime) and his slaying of Fafner the Dragon (hence the name 'Fafnersbane'). Then follows *Sigrdrifumál* (the *Lay of Sigrdrifa*), in which Sigurd finds and awakens a sleeping valkyrie named Sigrdrifa, who had been cast by Odin into a magic sleep as a punishment for having granted victory to the wrong man in battle. After relating this to Sigurd she imparts magic runes and advice to him.

We encounter Brynhild herself in the next poem, which is known as *Brot av Sigurdarkvidu* or 'part of the *Lay of Sigurd*', because only a portion of it survives; how large a portion is missing may be judged by the length of another, later poem devoted to the same theme, *Sigurdarkvida en skamma* or the *Short Lay of Sigurd*, so-called to distinguish it from the earlier lay. Since *Skamma* is in fact one of the longest surviving poems of the *Edda*, one can assume that *Brot* was even longer still and thus contained more material; the true extent of this unfortunate loss (the latter part of *Sigrdrifumál* is also affected) will be realised as our study progresses and we encounter several still unanswered questions about certain events in the *Edda*. The gist of the story can be filled in from other, later poems which incorporate prophecies or recapitulations of events already described in older poems: *Gripisspá (Griper's Prophecies)* and the various lays of Gudrun are such poems, as is *Skamma* itself; one problem, of course, is that it cannot be assumed that the story as presented in such poems coincides exactly with the versions in older, now missing portions of poems.

The broad outlines of the story would appear to be as follows. Sigurd, continuing his journey after awakening Sigrdrifa, meets Brynhild at the court of a chieftain and falls in love with her. They swear oaths to each other and Sigurd gives Brynhild a gold ring. Thereafter he arrives at King Giuki's court (Gibich in *Götterdämmerung*) and is ensnared by Queen Grimhild into marrying their daughter Gudrun (Wagner's Gutrune). He swears an oath of brotherhood to his new brothers-in-law Gunnar (Gunther) and Hogni (Hagen, who here is a full brother of Gunnar), and later he changes appearances with Gunnar in order to win Brynhild as the latter's wife. Brynhild, eventually realising that she has been betrayed, urges Gunnar to murder Sigurd. The deed is carried out by another younger brother, Guttorm, who, like Hagen in *Götterdämmerung*, is free to act because he has not participated in the oaths with Sigurd.

*Skamma* begins with Sigurd's marriage to Gudrun. One of the most recent poems of the *Edda*, it was first set down in the thirteenth century. The material differs in some details from what survives of *Brot*, chiefly in that the murder is committed, not outdoors 'south of the Rhine' (the outdoor tradition being more prevalent), but at home, in the marriage bed. The poem ends with Brynhild's prophecy of future events, her request that her body and Sigurd's be burnt together, and her suicide.

The most important of the subsequent poems is *Atlakvida* or the *Song of Atli*, 'in its archaic brutality and unbridled heroism one of the absolute high points of heroic poetry'.[9] It is based on the conflation of two historical events: the destruction of the Burgundian kingdom on the Rhine by a Hunnish army in 436, and the death of Attila seventeen years later during his wedding feast with a German (rumour had it, Burgundian) princess. These two events are linked in the poem by a revenge motive: Attila's bride, traditionally called Hildiko, becomes the sister of the fallen Burgundian kings, and she is said to have murdered Attila in revenge for the deaths of her kinsmen.[10] To Attila, or Atli, is attributed the motive of greed: coveting the Burgundian treasure, he invites Gunnar and Hogni to visit the Hun court. Hogni, ever the counsellor of caution, warns against the visit, pointing out the ring entwined with wolf's hair that Gudrun, their sister and the wife of Atli, has sent with Atli's message as a sign of warning. Gunnar will not be dissuaded from the journey, however, for it does not befit a king to turn away from danger, whether real or apparent. Upon their arrival at the Hun court Gunnar and Hogni are captured, bound and challenged to buy their lives by revealing the whereabouts of their famed treasure. They each refuse to do so and thus meet their deaths. Gudrun, to avenge her brothers, prepares and serves Atli a meal which, after he has consumed it, she reveals to have been the hearts of their two young sons. That night she sets fire to the hall and burns the sleeping Hun king and all his men to death.

The essential story of *Atlakvida* must have been the substance of the original lay of the Burgundian defeat. In the area south of Lake Geneva, where the Burgundians who survived the massacre of 436 had resettled, occurred much mixture of Eastern and Germanic cultures, and in the Eddic poem there are a number of elements of a decidedly Mediterranean influence, above all such gruesome details as the cutting out of hearts, snake pits and the eating of one's children. Thus the original lay must have come from the Burgundians themselves, and in this form it would have reached Scandinavia towards the end of the eighth century;

*Atlakvida* itself probably dates from about 870.[11]

Noteworthy about the poem is the way in which the action has been reduced from dissension between nations – Burgundians *vs*. Huns – to strife between individuals – Gunnar and Hogni *vs*. Atli. This recalls the earlier-mentioned tendency of the first lays to focus on the particular rather than the general, and is typical of the Nordic, as opposed to the Germanic, Nibelung tradition.

In the Codex Regius a note appended to *Atlakvida* informs that the story is told in greater detail in the Greenlandic *Atlamál*. The latter poem indeed relates the same events as *Atlakvida* but in a much more detailed and drawn-out fashion. There is a striking contrast between the primitive starkness of the earlier poem and the loquaciousness of the latter. 'It is as if heroic poetry had sunk to a more everyday level, both socially and esthetically.'[12] Nevertheless it will be seen later that even *Atlamál* was not without influence on Wagner when he wrote the poem of *The Ring*.

From the relatively brief poems of the *Edda* we turn to the lengthy mediaeval epics: one Nordic, one German and the third a blend of the two. The *Volsunga Saga*, composed by an anonymous author in Iceland around 1275, relates the history of the Volsung race from its founder, the god Odin, to Aslaug, daughter of Sigurd. Steeped in primeval accounts of gods and other mythical figures, the VS forms the major source not only for the Wälsungs in *Die Walküre* but also for many of the purely mythical figures in *The Ring*.[13]

The first part of the saga relates the events up to Sigurd's birth after the death of Sigmund, while the second part concerns itself with Sigurd's life and death, the downfall of the Giukungs at the hands of Atli, and the subsequent fate of Gudrun and her sons. In this part a direct prose paraphrase of the heroic poems of the *Edda* – the poems with parallel contents being combined – forms the backbone of the narrative which, as expected, affords a more detailed treatment of the events than do the poems. With the help of the VS it has been possible to fill in the gaps in the *Edda* narration arising from missing pages in the Codex Regius. In the VS survives information about Sigurd's winning of Brynhild which we would otherwise not have. Further, the saga describes at greater length Grimhild's machinations to wed Gudrun to Sigurd and enlist the latter's aid in wooing Brynhild for Gunnar; here figures Grimhild's magic drink which erases Sigurd's memory of Brynhild, while Sigurd's marriage to Gudrun is bound up with his being granted a share in Gunnar's dominion and the swearing of a brotherhood oath. Also elaborated upon in the saga is the enmity between Brynhild and Gudrun which culminates in the quarrel over the status of their respective husbands: this quarrel is a pivotal incident in the saga, for in the course of it is revealed that not Gunnar, but Sigurd in Gunnar's guise, rode the flames to woo Brynhild, a revelation which ultimately brings about Sigurd's downfall.

In contrast to the primeval VS stands the refined and cultivated Middle High German epic, the *Nibelungenlied*, whose anonymous author was 'probably one of the better sort of professional entertainers who in addition to their varied talents had learned to read and write after some measure of clerical education'.[14] The work was composed around the year 1200, for a court on or near the Danube, somewhere between Vienna and Passau. The epic follows Siegfried's arrival at the court of Gunther from the home of his parents, King Siegmund and Queen Sieglinde of the Netherlands, his conquest, in a series of sporting games, of Brunhild for Gunther in exchange for the hand of the latter's sister Kriemhild (here the sister has the Germanised form of the mother's name Grimhild in the Nordic sources); the quarrel between Brunhild and Kriemhild in which the latter reveals that not Gunther but Siegfried had taken Brunhild's virginity; Siegfried's murder by Hagen for that offence; the wresting of Siegfried's treasure from Kriemhild and its sinking in the Rhine River; Kriemhild's subsequent marriage to King Etzel (=Attila or Atli) and finally her revenge on Gunther and Hagen for the death of Siegfried.

Some important variations between the Nordic and the South German traditions will be noted. First there is the attitude towards the king of Hunland, who in the Nordic tradition appears as the greedy, bloodthirsty Atli, and in the South German tradition as the benevolent Etzel. The reasons for this difference lie in the relations of the different tribes during the Migration Period with the Hun leader Attila who is the most important historical model for Atli/Etzel. To the Germanic tribes in the west, from whose early lays the Nordic tradition eventually developed, Attila was a dreaded despot, while to the South Germans were handed down favourable memories of him from his allies, the Ostrogoths. This difference involves an important change in the motive for the invitation of the Burgundians to Hunland and their subsequent deaths: while in the Nordic sources it is Atli who invites them out of greed for the treasure, in the German it is their sister who does so in order to avenge her murdered husband Siegfried, while Etzel remains an innocent bystander.

The difference between the Nordic and the South German attitudes towards Attila also involves variations in their respective conceptions of the Hagen figure. In the Nordic version of the legend the downfall of the Giukungs has a straightforward cause, their betrayal by Atli who issues the treacherous invitation, then murders them when they do not accede to his demands for the treasure. However, the favourable South German concept of Etzel precluded the attachment of the 'betrayal' theme – which is an integral factor in the Burgundian downfall – to him; thus it had to become associated with another character. Essentially that character was Kriemhild, who sends for the Burgundians out of a desire both to avenge Siegfried and to recover his treasure; inevitably, however, in view of Etzel's lack of a traitor image, that image would attach itself to another figure whose historical antecedents were the same as, or intimately related to, Etzel's, and that figure was Hagen. This latter state of affairs will be examined in due course, but for now it should be noted that it is essentially Hagen who is the object of Kriemhild's fury, Hagen who has murdered her first husband and caused the treasure to be hidden in the Rhine. All Hagen had to do was to walk out and offer himself to Kriemhild's avenging sword and everyone else would have been saved; his refusal to do so, however, necessitated the holocaust in which all the Burgundians lost their lives. Thus it is to Hagen that many commentators[15] attribute the essential responsibility for the Burgundian defeat in the NL. Intimately linked with this important role is Hagen's enjoyment of the influential position in which we know him in *The Ring*, that of indispensable adviser to the king and power behind the throne, a position which, as we have seen, he does not fully hold in the Nordic sources.

A further difference between the two traditions is that in the Scandinavian account of the Burgundian defeat the emphasis in the strife, despite the presence and participation of the retinues of the respective antagonists, is between individuals – Gunnar and Hogni on one side and Atli on the other – while in the South German entire peoples are involved: the entire Burgundian complement of warriors travels to Hunland and is destroyed to the last man in a terrible bloody conflict with King Etzel's army. This is possibly a reflection of the era in which the NL was composed. 'Knighthood was in flower' and the poet may have been catering to his audience's predilection for crowd scenes: not only ferocious battles but also colourful scenes of pageantry with ladies in splendid dresses and mounted men in their regalia. Even the nature of the women's quarrel is affected by the NL's emphasis on the general or impersonal rather than the particular or personal. The feud in the VS, although initiated by a heated difference of opinion over whose husband is bravest, essentially concerns which of the two women has the greater right to Sigurd (Brynhild having sworn to wed only the bravest of men), and thus it is an intensely personal matter, involving as it does Brynhild's recollection of the vows of love sworn between Sigurd and herself and, in turn, Gudrun's complete lack of concern over those vows. In the NL, on the other hand, the quarrel is essentially political: arising from Brunhild's misconception that Siegfried is Gunther's vassal, it concentrates on the matter of the respective royal status of the two husbands; only when Kriemhild produces what she believes to be the evidence for Siegfried's defloration of Brunhild and thus his insult of her for having revealed the fact, is a personal element brought in.

On a deeper level is possibly the poet's desire to convey a message for the times in which he lived:

> The NL poet's political message, in his age of the power dispute between Philip of Swabia and Otto of Brunswick which was splitting the kingdom, was an appeal to peace and reason, to law and contracts. By depicting the fearful destruction of a nation he shows that when political murders are committed and uncontrolled revenge is rampant, there can be no order and the innocent die with the guilty. [16]

The era of the NL was, too, a Christian era. Gone are the old gods and virtually any other element of pagan myth; Brunhild is no valkyrie but a super-powerful amazon to be won, not through braving magic fire but by being bested at a series of athletic contests, and indeed the description of the competition between her and Gunther, in which the invisible Siegfried really performs the feats while Gunther goes through the motions, assumes a farcical nature. Moreover, any admission of a prior acquaintance between Siegfried and Brunhild is omitted, although some parts of the plot appear to hint at such an acquaintance. Another mythical element of the legend, Siegfried's slaying of the dragon, does not actually occur within the action of the poem but is recounted by Hagen. The old Teutonic religion of Odin (Wotan) is replaced by Christianity; the quarrel between Kriemhild and Brunhild takes place in front of the Cathedral, and Hagen exhorts his men to attend Mass on the morning they will fight the Huns.

The thirteenth-century *Thidrekssaga*, or *Vilkina Saga*, combines the Scandinavian and the German branches of the

Nibelung legend, having been compiled in Norway from the oral tradition of the Westphalian area, above all from Soest, Bremen and Münster, from material supplied by North German merchants. The chief hero, Thidrek or Didrik of Bern, is historically Theodorich, king of the Ostrogoths, conqueror of Italy, whose seats of power were Ravenna and Verona (= Bern) and who died in 526. That a pre-existing Scandinavian tradition of Theodorich or Didrik could have influenced the material received from Westphalia is not inconceivable; the Eddic poems tell of King Tjodrek who visits Atli and Gudrun, and a verse on a Swedish rune stone at Rök in Östergötland dating from *ca.* 830 mentions 'Didrik den stormodige vid Hreidhavets strand': 'Didrik the proud at the shore of Hreid Sea'. Of specific interest to the Wagnerian is that the lengthy prose saga also included the history of Sigurd and the Burgundians. Here the two different motives for destroying the Burgundians (who in this saga are called 'Niflungs' = Nibelungs) are combined: Grimhild (= Kriemhild of the NL or Gudrun of the *Edda* and VS) asks Attila to invite her brothers to visit, ostensibly to gain back Sigurd's treasure from him, which she will share with him in return for his help, although actually revenge for Sigurd's death is her main motive; Attila agrees because he is greedy and lusts for gold. The story of Sigurd and the Niflungs is not self-contained, as in the VS, but interwoven with many other stories of different heroes; Didrik himself participates in the Niflungs' last stand at the court of Attila (as indeed he does in the NL under the name of 'Dietrich').

The Nibelung legend, as we now know it from the Eddic poems and the mediaeval epics, evolved from two legends that originally were totally independent of each other: on the one hand, the legend of Siegfried, his slaying of the dragon, winning of the treasure and winning of Brunhild; and on the other, the downfall of the Burgundians and the death of its perpetrator, Attila, in revenge. The evolution of the Nibelung legend will now be summarised in terms of the process of combination of these two originally separate stories, for, as we shall see later, this dual evolution of the legend has left important traces on the make-up of the different characters involved.

The destruction of the Rhenish Burgundian kingdom by Hunnish troops led to the early lays on the fall of the Burgundians. (In the *Ring Cycle* this corresponds to the death of Gunther and the physical destruction of his court.) Somewhat later, the death of Attila through haemorrhage during nuptials with his German bride gave rise to the story that his wife murdered him. The two were then combined: Attila was made responsible for the Burgundian downfall (with greed for their treasure being made the motive) and his wife, who had now become a Burgundian princess, murders him to avenge the deaths of her kin. This, then, comprised one half of the Nibelung legend.

The date of the earliest version of the Siegfried legend is difficult to establish. Some scholars, dating the origins of the Siegfried legend from the time of the Frankish king and queen Sigebert and Brunechild, claim that the Burgundian half is earlier, as the historical events enshrined therein precede the reign of Sigebert; however, the origin of the Siegfried legend is in fact not so simple, and its roots reach back considerably farther than the Migration Period, if we accept that originally the protagonists did not have their present names.[17] One can assume that up to the sixth century the legend had been expanded with features that did not essentially alter the original story. Then, around that time two important things happened: the Siegfried legend was influenced by historical events in the sixth-century Merovingian kingdom, and it became intermingled with the Burgundian legend. Both of these occurrences had far-reaching effects on the subsequent development of the Siegfried legend.

Why would the Siegfried legend have become interwoven

with the Burgundian/Attila legend at all? The following possible reasons present themselves:

1.  A similarity between the original name of Siegfried's wife and the name of the Burgundians' sister with whom she became identified.[18]  This is a purely hypothetical explanation, since the original name of Siegfried's wife is not known at all.

2.  The similarity between the historical name Nibelung (thought to be the dynastic name of the Rhenish Burgundian royal family) and the mythical name of Siegfried's murderers.[19] However, some scholars[20] believe that the name 'Nibelung' was first and foremost an historical one and that the mythical connotations of beings associated with darkness and fog developed not parallel with the historical name, but later, from it.

3.  Circumstances in the life of the historical Frankish king Sigebert that could have bridged events in both of the legends. For example, besides his obvious associations with the Siegfried legend, he also had a brother whose name, Guntram, resembled that of the Burgundian king Gundahari (= Gunther), and with whom his relations were not always the friendliest.[21]

4.  The identification of Siegfried's treasure with the treasure for which Attila destroyed the Burgundians. These last two possibilities are the most likely ones.

It is noteworthy that no Eddic poems on Sigurd's murder are now extant which do not presuppose a connection with the Burgundian legend, in the form of Brynhild's prophecy of retribution on the Burgundians (or Giukungs or Niflungs as they are called). In both *Brot* and *Skamma* Brynhild, on the verge of killing herself after Sigurd's murder, accuses them of breaking their oaths of loyalty to Sigurd and foretells that the Giukungs will suffer retribution for this perfidy. These poems are more recent – in the latter case considerably so – than *Atlakvida* which treats the Giukungs' downfall and Atli's subsequent death, and which is completely self-contained with no mention of the slightest aspect of the Sigurd story. It must be stressed that greed for the treasure is still Atli's personal reason for doing away with the Giukungs; the retribution for Sigurd's death, foretold by Brynhild in the Sigurd lays, is not Atli's conscious intention but the working of fate, of impersonal justice: Atli is interested only in the treasure, not in avenging a death that occurred in a different lay.

The brother–sister relationship between Atli and Brynhild, occurring in *Skamma* but not mentioned in *Atlakvida*, would seem to be another bridging method between the two halves of the legend, and one closely associated with the connecting device of the prophecies, of which device the poet, from his vantage point at the late stage of Eddic creation, was able to avail himself. By providing this family link – letting a prominent character (Brynhild) in the first half of the legend become close kin of the protagonist of the second half (Atli) – one could convincingly put the prophecy of retribution into Brynhild's mouth.

Connected with and following from this is the motive of sister-vengeance: Atli's desire to avenge the death of Brynhild as a reason for stirring up hostilities towards the Giukungs. To be sure, the 'sister-vengeance' theme is not lacking in historical precedent, having been crucial to Merovingian history (*cf.* Chapter Three). However, since it obviously does not occur in *Atlakvida* this motive is no more a part of the original story than is the retribution on the Giukungs for their perfidy towards Sigurd; rather it is 'tacked on' in the later *Atlamál* to link the two halves of the legend more closely, and incorporated into the VS when Atli says to the Giukungs: 'You have wasted my kin and cheated me of my wealth; but what grieves me most of all is that you have slain my sister.' But this is an obvious pretext on Atli's part, as the reaction to this accusation would indicate:

> What do you have to complain about? It was you who first broke the peace. You murdered my mother for her riches, and let my kinswoman starve to death in a cave. I think it's ridiculous that you should complain of your sorrows, and I thank the gods that

things are going bad for you. [22]

Another factor which had bearing on the merging of the two legends was the difference between the Northern and the South German traditions with respect to their views of Attila. As the North regarded Attila as a villain who lusted after power and wealth, the Burgundians are destroyed through his greed for their treasure. However, the South German tradition, having arisen in areas occupied by former allies of the Huns, had a favourable picture of Attila as the kindly King Etzel; accordingly the Burgundians meet their end at the hands of a vengeful Kriemhild. The Northern was the earlier version because the legend originated among Frankish or Burgundian peoples with whom Attila was unpopular; this version, moreover, was self-contained, while the avenging-sister motive depended on incorporation from the Siegfried legend. Thus in the process of connecting both halves of the legend one other problem had to be solved, that of explaining why Gudrun did *not* take revenge on her brothers for the slaying of Sigurd, and why in fact she even attempted to warn them about the treacherous nature of Atli's invitation. This was done by allowing Gudrun's mother to give her a magic drink which erased Gudrun's memory of her brothers' perfidy towards Sigurd. This is described in *Gudrunarkvida II* (the *Second Lay of Gudrun*) and has also been incorporated into Brynhild's prophecy in *Skamma*, one of the youngest Eddic poems.

To sum up, then, the process of mutual incorporation of the two halves of the Nibelung legend can be outlined as follows:

1. Early versions of what later became the Siegfried legend.
2. Lays on downfall of the Burgundians.
3. Lays on the death of Attila, incorporating his 'murder' by his German bride.
4. Combination of 2 and 3:
    *a.* Attila is made responsible for the downfall of the Burgundians. Motive for destroying them: his greed for their treasure.

*b.* Revenge motive: wife kills Attila to avenge the deaths of her Burgundian kin.

5. Historical influences on Siegfried legend: protagonists acquire definitive names, Siegfried and Brunhild.

6. Further historical influences on Siegfried legend and its combination with the legend of the Burgundian downfall and death of Attila:

    *a.* Siegfried's marriage to the Burgundian royal sister and swearing of loyalty oaths to her kin;

    *b.* Burgundians become identified as Siegfried's murderers, slaying him for infidelity to the oaths;

    *c.* chief device connecting the two legends; fate – retribution by impersonal justice for Burgundians' murder of Siegfried, through Attila's perpetration of their downfall – comes into the Siegfried poems in the form of Brunhild's prophecy of their downfall;

    *d.* subordinate bridging device: Brunhild becomes Attila's sister in order to foretell the Burgundians' downfall (retribution);

    *e.* problem of consistency solved: question of why Gudrun does not avenge Siegfried's murder explained by letting her take magic drink of forgetfulness;

    *f.* reconciliation between Gudrun and her brothers also incorporated into Brunhild's prophecies in the Sigurd poems.

## Notes

1. *Agricola*, pp. 91ff.

2. *Germania*, p. 129.

3. Berndt, p. 71.

4. Mone, p. 3.

5. Nack, p. 123.

6.  *Germania*, p. 103.

7.  Nack, p. 225.

8.  Berndt, p. 52.

9.  Hallberg, p. 81.

10. In actual fact Attila was not murdered but died of a haemorrhage, nor was he present at the battle of 436.

11. *Die Edda* (Genzmer), p. 28.

12. Hallberg, p. 84.

13. This is discussed in exhaustive detail by Deryck Cooke, in *I Saw the World End*, which also gives a complete summary of the VS.

14. *The Nibelungenlied*, p. 293.

15. most notably Hatto, p. 319.

16. Wapnewski, p. 125.

17. While 'Brynhild' and its variations derive from the sixth-century Frankish queen, it will be seen in Chapter Two that 'Siegfried' and so forth may be somewhat older.

18. Midderhoff.

19. Ljungstedt, p. 219.

20. Notably Mone, whose work Wagner acknowledged as one of the sources for the *Ring Cycle*.

21. A detailed discussion will be devoted to this aspect in later chapters.

22. In the VS these words are uttered by Hogni. The Codex Regius version of *Atlamál* indicates no particular speaker, although some translations, notably Ljungstedt and Collinder, assign them to Gudrun.

# 2

# The Hero in All His Glory

In *A Communication to My Friends* (1851) Wagner described how the character of Siegfried gradually unfolded before him:

> My studies drew me on, through the ancient poems of the middle ages, right back to the foundations of the ancient German mythology; I was able to strip away one distorting veil after another which later poetry had thrown over it, and so set eyes on it at last in all its chaste beauty . . . Although the splendid figure of Siegfried had long attracted me, he only fully enthralled me for the first time when I had succeeded in freeing him from all his later trappings, and saw him before me in his purest human form. It was then for the first time, too, that I recognised the possibility of making him the hero of a drama, which had never occurred to me while I knew him only from the mediaeval *Nibelungenlied*. [1]

Siegfried, as we know him from Wagner's tetralogy, enjoys a widespread reputation as a great and fearless hero and the possessor of a renowned treasure. In the course of the *Ring Cycle* we witness on stage two of Siegfried's greatest deeds: the slaying of the dragon Fafner by which he gains possession of the Nibelung ring, symbol of world dominion, and the Nibelung treasure; and the winning of Brünnhilde through braving the fire that surrounds the rock on which she sleeps. But he appears to have committed still other acts of heroism, presumably between the end of *Siegfried* and Act I of *Götterdämmerung*, which are not specifically mentioned or dramatised but are alluded to at various points during *Götterdämmerung*. For example, Brünnhilde hints to Hagen

(*Götterdämmerung*, Act II) that Siegfried has continued the warrior tradition of his father Siegmund:

Hagen:　　　　So can no weapon harm him?

Brünnhilde:　　Not in battle: but if you strike him in the back . . .
　　　　　　　never, that much I know, would he retreat from an
　　　　　　　　enemy,
　　　　　　　never would he flee and turn his back to him:
　　　　　　　so there I withheld my spells.

The exact nature of these deeds is not important: what does matter is that these allusions emphasise and reinforce Wagner's conception of Siegfried as an outstanding hero, a conception which can be traced back through the literary sources for the *Ring Cycle* to recorded history.

The earliest historical forbears for the heroic Siegfried stem from the Germanic tribes during the early years of the Roman Empire: brave and respected men who assumed leadership when conflicts arose in the often stormy relations between Rome and the German nations. One of these was *Arminius*, or Hermann, a chieftain of the Germanic Cherusci tribe during the reign of Augustus. Roman legions, under the leadership of P. Quinctilius Varus, had been sent to bring the tribes in north Germany under the Roman yoke. Arminius organised the Cherusci, along with some neighbouring tribes, to resist the Romans; however, he himself was opposed by a faction within his own tribe, led by his father-in-law Segestes, who believed that they would be better off allied to the Romans; if they remained free, it was thought, they would be condemned to poverty. Segestes had other, personal reasons for animosity towards Arminius: the young chieftain had abducted and married Segestes' daughter Thusnelda, although she had been promised by her father to someone else. Segestes continuously plotted against Arminius, even warning Varus of Arminius's plans; Varus, however, refused to take the warnings seriously.

Consequently he and his three legions were resoundingly defeated in a battle in the Teutoburg Forest in 9 A.D. Augustus gave up any further attempts to Romanise Germany, and Arminius became regarded as the Father of the German Nation. Thereafter, wishing to use his military successes to achieve political power, he aimed at becoming king of the Cherusci. Perhaps his ambition had reached too far too early: having then just achieved the kingship in 19 A.D., at the age of 37, he was assassinated, a victim of his relatives' conspiracy.

Some sixty years later one *C. Julius Civilis*, a Batavian chieftain, rose to prominence. The Batavians, a tribe occupying part of a Roman province on the Rhine, were obliged to supply the Roman army with auxiliary troops, the leaders of which came from among the nobles of the tribe. During the confusion that reigned after the death of the Emperor Nero, when several contenders vied for the Imperial throne, Civilis was prefect of the Batavian auxiliaries. When Vitellius was proclaimed Emperor by the legions on the Rhine and Vespasian by the troops in the East the auxiliaries under Civilis started an insurrection against Vitellius, because he had not only given them marching orders for Italy instead of re-posting them to Britain as they had hoped and expected, but had also levied tributes on the tribe, from which they had formerly been exempt. Because of its initial success what had begun as a revolt of auxiliary troops against their legions snowballed into an attempt by the Batavians and their neighbouring tribes to shake off Roman rule and proclaim their independence; all but two of the legionary camps and fortresses fell, and the Roman fleet on the Rhine fell into Batavian hands. Eventually, however, the hostilities reached a stalemate; the Germans grew tired of war and members of Civilis' own family had been taken into Roman hands. Civilis negotiated with the representatives of Vespasian and it was agreed to restore the conditions prevailing prior to the insurrection.

A relatively minor Siegfried forbear was the martyr *St. Victor of Xanten*, a city now near the German-Dutch border.

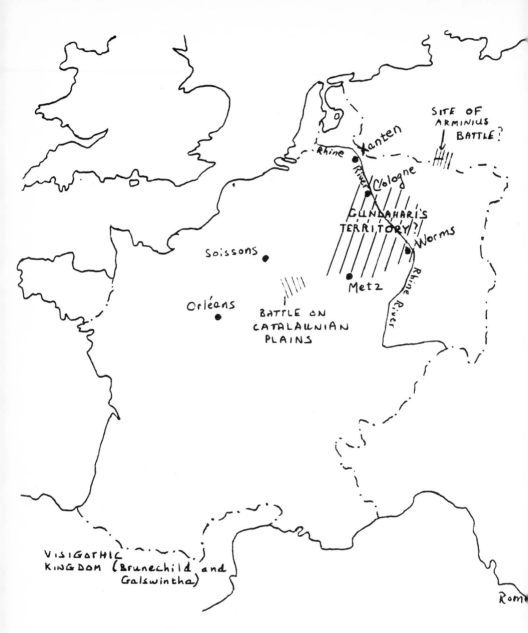

SITE OF ARMINIUS BATTLE?

Rhine

Xanten

Cologne

GUNDAHARI'S TERRITORY?

Worms

Rhine River

Soissons

Metz

Orléans

BATTLE ON CATALAUNIAN PLAINS

VISIGOTHIC KINGDOM (Brunechild and Galswintha)

Rome

— · — — · — Frankish kingdom at time of Sigebert, Guntram and Chilperich.

Metz = Sigebert's capital
Orléans = Guntram's "
Soissons = Chilperich's "

**MAP OF HISTORICAL EVENTS.**

According to local Xanten legend Victor was captain of a Roman legion around the beginning of the fourth century; as he and his troops were Christians they refused to sacrifice to the Roman gods and were thereupon all slain, and the bodies supposedly buried just outside Xanten.[2] The association of this place with martyr-saints gave the city its present name, for 'Xanten' is a corruption of '(Civitas) ad Sanctos' or 'City of the Saints'.

Since the name 'Victor' is the Latin equivalent of 'Siegfried' people in fairly recent times have come to equate the two figures. In fact the chief part played by the Victor legend in the Siegfried story seems to have been the confirmation of Xanten as Siegfried's birthplace. The association between Siegfried and Xanten is thought to have begun with songs and ballads of Arminius which were preserved by the German auxiliary troops stationed at the Roman army camp of Castra Vetera (today Xanten) and to which some forms of the Siegfried legend are believed to be able in part to trace their ancestry. Civilis too gave the troops at Xanten reason to remember him, for in the course of the Batavian onslaught the Rhenish legions were repulsed back to, and surrounded in, Castra Vetera. It is thought that this identification of Xanten with the earlier Siegfried forbears, along with other features shared by the Saint and the hero – the similarity between the name, and the slaying of dragons, for such Germanic heroes who defied the might of Rome are often depicted as dragon slayers[3] – can have inspired the NL poet to localise his hero there.

In the careers of such men as Arminius and Julius Civilis can be recognised several elements that run like a red thread through the fabric of heroic legend. They were *great military heroes* and *leaders of their nations*: Tacitus called Arminius 'liberator of Germany'.[4] Further, 'Arminius' most likely was not a proper name but a kind of title meaning 'the great': the ancient form would have been Erminiaz. Most likely his real name began with 'Sig–' in conformity with the other male members of his family, as was customary at that time: his father was called Sigimer, his uncle Sigimund.

The fame of Arminius and Civilis was long enshrined in the memory of the German people. Of Arminius Tacitus reported, 'Barbarian peoples still sing his praises today,'[5] that is, nearly one hundred years after his death. Even during the nineteenth century Arminius was taken up as a symbol of the movement for German nationalism and unity. Artistic works devoted to him proliferated. Not only did poems and paintings immortalise him but so did at least one opera: *Die Hermannsschlacht (The Battle of Arminius)*, performed in Munich[6] when its composer, Hippolyte Chélard, was Kapellmeister there. However, the most famous monument to Arminius from this period is the gigantic statue which still stands proudly on a mountain top near Detmold, close to what is believed to have been the site of his battle against Varus. The life's work of its designer Ernst von Bandel, the 'Hermann Monument' had as its artistic theme

> not a similarity with the historical personality of Arminius but his gesture of raising the sword, which represents that German unity and power with which he chastised the Roman Empire. [7]

The historical figures who became celebrated in heroic legend were men who *met a challenge*, who *fought for an ideal*. That is what made them heroes, what constituted their appeal to the popular imagination. Their lives have been handed down as a series of mythical or legendary deeds played out against a background tapestry of historical or semi-historical events. But how does history become legend? By what process are ballads of Arminius transformed into the legend of Siegfried?

In the early nineteenth century the discipline of Germanic philology was in its infancy. Inevitably misunderstandings arose, errors were made. For example, it was not uncommon to seek the historical origins of a legendary figure in a single historical personage and then reject the possibility of such origins, because the correspondences between legendary character and historical person were not exact. Such an error was due to a lack of understanding of the process by which historical material was assimilated into legend. One of the first to get it right was Franz Joseph Mone. He recognised that a character in a heroic saga derives not from one historical personage but from several.

> The historical character of a heroic saga consists, not in its individual and true depiction of historical persons (for then it would be a history), but in that it extracts from the lives of such persons those occurrences and features that lend themselves to the established picture of their heroes. [8]

Thus, for example, the legend assimilates and emphasises those common features of the historical personages which fit the pattern for that particular character, whether it be hero, villain, betrayed wife or weak king.

In the case of a heroic figure like Siegfried, for example, such characteristics as noble or royal origins and brave deeds have survived from historical persons like Arminius for assimilation into the legend. Siegfried's *close connection with royalty* is a feature common to all the extant sources. In the VS Sigurd's father, Sigmund, is king in the land of the Huns, and Sigurd himself is born in Denmark at the court of the Danish king; however, he does not exercise any royal power through his natural inheritance but only, as in the Ths. too, through his marriage to Gunnar's sister. In the VS he holds dominion as a prince of Giuki's land through his marriage, while in the Ths. he receives half of Gunnar's kingdom as dowry and thereby becomes co-ruler of Werniza (Worms) with Gunnar. Only in the NL does Siegfried enjoy any inherited royal suzerainty: after his marriage to Kriemhild the couple return to his native Netherlands, to the great city of Xanten, where his father 'made over to his son his crown, his judicature, and his kingdom. From now on Siegfried was their supreme lord'.

Siegfried's *heroic deeds* – the 'neuen Taten' to which Wagner's Brünnhilde encourages him – would appear, in the terse poetry of the *Edda*, to be implied by the references to his leader status: one would hardly expect such epithets as 'king of heroes' *(Brot)* or 'War-lord of the Danes' *(Brynhild's Ride to Hel)* to have been meant literally as titles of military or political suzerainty. In the more extensive epic works, however, Siegfried's heroism is further elaborated upon by the depiction of specific deeds of bravery. In the NL, for example, Siegfried's help is indispensable to the Burgundians' victory over the Saxons and Danes. Kriemhild's messenger enthusiastically reports to her:

> From beginning to end of the battle, Siegfried did the greatest deeds that were ever witnessed anywhere – and with what relish! The splendid man is bringing back to Gunther's land captives of great rank, subdued by his strength and courage, for whom King Liudegast and his brother Liudeger of Saxony must bear the loss. And . . .Siegfried captured them both! Thanks to his prowess, never were so many prisoners brought back to this country as are coming Rhinewards now![9]

The Ths. similarly reviews many campaigns and battles in which Sigurd participates alongside Didrik, the main hero of the epic, and the VS relates how Sigurd and the Giukungs

> now travelled widely throughout the lands and did many a brave deed; they slew many kings' sons, and no other men accomplished such wonderful things as they did . . .

What is the driving force behind heroic legend that assimilates some bits of historical information, discards others, and transposes and juxtaposes all into a pattern without regard for the original details of time and place? What, in other words, ultimately constitutes 'the established picture of . . . heroes' to which historical figures and events are made to conform in legend?

The answer, says Mone, is myth.

> The saga differs from history in that the saga assimilates the historical material according to the ideas of the myth, while history must adhere strictly to the causality of events. [10]

Thus when details of individual persons and events became obfuscated with time, the sagas began to assume the shape of familiar mythical themes. Siegfried – and Brunhild too – are no exception. In the course of their legendary lives the relationship between historical and mythical elements is constantly shifting, thus providing a richness of influences that had no small import for Wagner's interpretation of the characters.

It is above all in the Scandinavian tradition that Sigurd exhibits the typical features of a timeless mythical hero. One such feature involves some form of mysterious parentage. In the *Edda* and VS Sigurd's father, King Sigmund, dies before his son's birth and his mother Hjördis gives him to be brought up by a foster-father, Regin the smith. In the Ths. Sigurd begins life in a similar fashion: there he is the son of King Sigmund of Tarlungland and Sisibe, daughter of the King of Spain. Put into a pot by his mother he floats downstream until he reaches the sea; upon being washed up on shore he is suckled by a doe until found and reared by Mimi the smith.[11]

Another prominent accoutrement of mythical heroes the world over is the slaying of a dragon, and with this the acquisition of a treasure or the rescuing of a woman in the dragon's thrall. The dragon-slaying episode is an important example of the interaction of history and myth in the Siegfried legend. Throughout the world and from time immemorial such a deed has been an allegorical expression of a hero's overcoming of some obstacle or his victory over an enemy; it was firmly established as such long before the historical forebears for our Siegfried walked the earth.

In his brilliant study of mythology Joseph Campbell[12] includes an illustration of a twelfth-century Chinese scroll depicting a dragon clutching a glowing sphere. 'A pearl? The sun? In either case, a great treasure.' Chinese dragons are 'dangerous but benign. And in India too the "serpent kings" guard both the waters of immortality and the treasures of the earth.' That not only jewels and wealth, but also beautiful women are of interest to dragons, is testified to by the legend of Andromeda, whom Perseus saved from a sea monster, and the Japanese story of the dragon killed by the storm god Susano-O in order to save the eighth daughter of a couple whose first

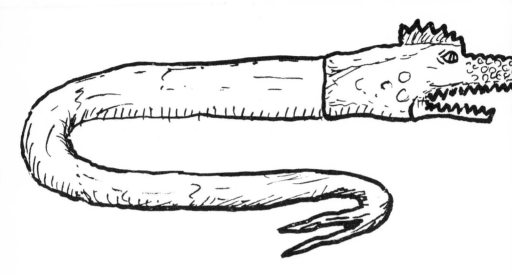

**Roman army standard with dragon head.**

seven had already been devoured.

Did the ballads of ancient Germanic heroes claim that the hero had slain a dragon? Quite possibly. The dominion of. Rome was often symbolised by a dragon, and indeed in the fourth and fifth centuries the Roman army standards were bronze dragon heads whose bodies were of cloth 'socks' that inflated in the wind. It is therefore entirely conceivable that the victory of Arminius over the might of Rome was symbolised in the popular imagination by his slaying of a dragon. Thus here the dragon-slaying symbolism functions on two levels: first, the universal mythical archetype as described above, and secondly the particular symbolisation of Roman might by the dragon which adorned their military standards. The dragon-slaying motif remained through all subsequent re-workings of the legend.

Intimately linked with mythical dragon-slaying is the treasure won by the hero through killing the dragon. In our Siegfried legend the treasure motif, like the dragon symbolism, functions on two levels: as a product of universal consciousness it is the reward won by a mythical hero, and in a more specific context it symbolises the (moral or tangible) results of a victory of a legendary hero who derives ultimately from historical models. Sometimes, too, the treasure as such derives from actual historical ones – one example in Siegfried's case is the Roman war booty taken by the forces of Arminius in the Teutoburg Forest – but the implications of the treasure will be treated at length in Chapter Seven.

With the dragon-slaying and treasure-winning motifs of the Siegfried legend, then, we have seen how universal-mythical and historico-legendary symbolism run parallel as the allegorical expression of historical events coincides with ancient, established mythical motifs. However, in the Siegfried legend are reflected not only universal and general mythical motifs but also specific figures from Germanic mythology.

Around 1,000 B.C. some Scandinavian tribes began pushing southwards until they reached the area of the Rhine and Main rivers by 200 B.C. and in the first century A.D. had occupied most of what is now southern Germany. A second migration from Scandinavia began around 500 B.C. with tribes crossing the Baltic into the regions of the Oder and Vistula rivers and then moving southwards to the Carpathian mountains until they reached the Black Sea between 250 and 150 B.C.

These migrations had considerable significance for the peoples left behind in Scandinavia. The emigrants' contact with the native peoples of their new lands – for example, the Greeks – resulted in the assimilation of new cultural and religious ideas, ideas which travelled back 'home' by way of migration and trade routes. It is thus not surprising, as Brian Branston comments, that 'religious conceptions and even gods and goddesses of Asia Minor and Egypt brought an exotic beam of the Middle Eastern sun to the cold northern latitudes'.[13]

Such an imported figure was Balder. He is not an original

Northwest European conception, but a reflection of such Mediterranean and Eastern figures as Tammuz and Ba'al which penetrated to Germany and the North via the amber trade routes.

The versions of Balder's life and death differ from source to source, but coincide on some points. The exact nature of the ancient Germanic conception of Balder is unclear: he seems to have had one foot in the world of gods and the other in the realm of human heroes. On the one hand, in Snorri's *Edda* and the sources on which Snorri builds his tale – the Eddic poems *Lokasenna (Loki's Quarrel), Balder's Dreams* and *Völuspá* – Balder is a god, the son of Odin, who consorts with the gods and after his death goes to Hel.[14] The Danish historian Saxo Grammaticus, on the other hand, records quite a different tale of Balder in his *Gesta Danorum*; there he is a hero, said to be a demi-god, who leads armies in southern Scandinavia and, like his Eddic counterpart, is killed by Höd or Hother. It is thus not surprising that some of his qualities should have become associated with Siegfried.

Common to both the Nordic and the Germanic Siegfried traditions in connection with the Balder myth are their conception of the hero as handsome and fair (Balder is called 'the Beautiful', with a shining white face and blonde hair; both the VS and NL devote extensive passages to similar, flattering descriptions of Sigurd/Siegfried), and their emphasis on the bloody wound dealt to him (*Völuspá* refers to Balder as the 'bleeding god'). Further, the Nordic tradition preserves the common descent from Odin, for just as Balder in the *Edda* is a son of Odin so is Sigurd descended from the god in the VS. Since the most remarkable aspect of the Balder myth, and that to which the closest parallels occur in the Siegfried legend, is his treacherous slaying, any further and more detailed discussion of Balder will be saved for Chapter Five.

Another mythical figure significant to the Siegfried legend is the god Freyr. Like Balder Freyr has roots in the Mediterranean and Near-Eastern regions. He was popular during the Migration Period and the most outstanding fertility god in Northern Europe in the later pagan period. Besides being a fertility god Freyr was worshipped as a *bringer of peace*; moreover, he 'inspired joy and devotion. Men rejoiced to share their possessions with him'.[15] One of the most important Freyr sources to relate to the Siegfried legend is the Eddic poem *Skirnismál (Lay of Skirnir)* which in its present form probably dates from 900–950,[16] and which some critics interpret as stemming from an old cult poem for a fertility rite. The poem concerns Freyr's wooing of the giantess Gerd, which brings us to another important aspect of Siegfried to have mythical overtones, his *winning of a bride*.

There is no historical precedent for the attribution of bravery to Siegfried's acquisition of a bride; the closest that history comes to it is Gregory of Tours' praise of the Merovingian King Sigebert (see Chapter Three) for choosing to wed the noble and gracious Brunechild, in contrast to the questionable types of women with whom his brothers were associating.[17] Why, then, does the Siegfried legend present the hero's winning of a bride as a heroic act? Because such a deed commonly occurred in myth, and specifically in the story of Freyr as recounted in *Skirnismál*. And since the wives of some of the historical Siegfried forbears were prominent or fascinating figures in themselves it was natural that an interesting bride-winning story, assuming the ancient mythical form of the rescue or awakening motif, should become attached to the legend of our hero. Further treatment of the bride-wooing, however, is more suitably left to the discussion of The Heroine in the next chapter.

Some of the early nineteeth-century German philologists mistakenly attempted to discover the *origins* of legendary figures in ancient myth and to trace their *evolution* from the mythical figures. In actual fact, however, the characters of heroic legend had completely separate origins from those of myth: Siegfried *as such* did not begin his existence as a fertility god. What happened was that broad similarities between mythical and legendary characters stimulated the drawing of closer parallels and the transference of some details from god to hero; details, forgotten or discarded from the lives of historical personages who served as models for the legends, were replaced with elements adapted from myth. It was not uncommon for an idea from a myth to be added to an historically-derived feature of a legend in order to enhance its interest; in the case of Siegfried, for example, to his marriage to Gunther or Gunnar's sister and, connected with it, the sharing in his realms, ideas derived essentially from history, is added the above-mentioned motif from the Freyr mythology that Gunther's family were *glad and proud* to have this arrangement that the renowned hero should share in their realms and marry their sister. Sometimes this process of transforming mythical into historico-legendary material was a natural and unconscious process, sometimes – as we shall see later – quite deliberate.

What Wagner sought in Siegfried was a pure, unadulterated hero. He envisioned his Siegfried first and foremost as someone destined from all time to be the greatest hero the world has known, and strove in *The Ring* to portray him as such. The essential deeds, those associated in the universal consciousness with a hero – the killing of the dragon, winning of a treasure and penetrating of fire to win a bride – assume a central place in Wagner's drama. However, he neither dramatises, nor specifically mentions in the text, any of the quasi-military exploits related in the lengthy epics, although several passages in the *Ring* text, as has already been shown, offer the scope for imagining such events to have taken place. His inclusion of Hagen's account to Gunther of the above-mentioned 'mythical' achievements of Siegfried – which comes from the NL where it replaces an actual depiction of them – serves the dramatic function of illustrating Hagen's knowledge and allowing him to impart it to Gunther and Gutrune, as well

as implying the possibility that Siegfried's accomplishments
have amounted to more than what we have actually seen on
stage:

> When he's gaily hunting around for adventures
> the world becomes a narrow forest for him.

As Wagner himself has related, the NL Siegfried exerted no
strong appeal for him; deprived of the entrapments of the
essentially mythical hero he lacked the qualities of universality
and timelessness essential to the type of hero Wagner wanted
for his drama, and except for the vast power and wealth heaped
upon him by the mediaeval Austro-Bavarian poet in evidence
of his sovereignty he rises little above the stereotyped 'knight in
shining armour' of that era. He stems not from a mysterious
background but from a glittering mediaeval court at which
both his natural parents, King Siegmund and Queen Sieglinde
of the Netherlands, still live. His slaying of the dragon, too, is
assigned a minor place, in accordance with the mediaeval
Christian poet's toning down of the inherently mythical aspects
of the story, in that it is not actually depicted but only related
retrospectively by Hagen in his brief account to Gunther of
Siegfried's past; moreover, it has no connection whatever with
his acquisition of the treasure: thus the mythical aspect of the
origin of the treasure is lost in the NL, replaced by one that can
be traced back to purely historical events.

Consequently, for his Siegfried figure and especially for his
early history Wagner turned to the Scandinavian sources, in
which Sigurd retained the typical features of a timeless
mythical hero's origin and youth. Wagner's Siegfried, like
Sigurd of the *Edda* and VS, grows up in the care of a foster-
father (Mime the dwarf smith), never having known either of
his real parents: his father Siegmund died before he was born
and his mother Sieglinde in childbirth. The slaying of Fafner,
the advice of the woodbird and his following of that advice are
all adapted from Eddic poems, chiefly *Fafnesmál (Lay of
Fafner)* and *Sigrdrifumál*.

Another important feature of Wagner's young Siegfried is

his identification with the Boy Who Knew No Fear, which is established immediately upon his first appearance on stage, when he playfully leads on a ferocious bear with which to frighten Mime. This youthful brashness is carried over into the adult Siegfried's personality with his challenging greeting to Gunther, 'Fight with me or be my friend,' a much mitigated version of the rude, bellicose entry of the NL Siegfried at Gunther's court, which shocks the refined Burgundians.

In one sense, then, the youthful achievements of Wagner's Siegfried are all the heroic deeds of Nordic and Germanic legend rolled into one, and yet essentially they are not a dramatic symbol for these deeds but a means of showing how Siegfried as a universal heroic figure transcends limitations of time and place; for Wagner the dragon slaying and, with it, the acquisition of the treasure, serve to identify Siegfried as an embodiment of the archetypal mythical hero. The many parallels between Balder and the legendary Siegfried are anything but coincidence, and, as can be expected, they exerted considerable influence on Wagner's working-out of his own version of the Siegfried story. Wagner, of course, was aware of the connection between the legendary Siegfried and ancient sun-god figures; the many philological works he read referred to it, and he himself mentions it in his essay *Die Wibelungen*.

The 'Balder' feature of most general importance to *The Ring* is the descent from Odin: Siegfried as Wotan's grandson, created to bring about a new order of peace in the world just as Balder was expected to return and reign in peace after the Ragnarök, is one significant link between the divine and the human worlds of the tetralogy. The ship in which Wagner's Siegfried undertakes his famous 'Rhine journey' comes directly from Balder's ship Hringhorni on which his funeral pyre is burned, and even Siegfried's funeral pyre, inherited ultimately from Balder through the Nordic Sigurd, denotes him as a great hero, for in the real life of those peoples who cherished these legends – in the Viking Age and earlier – this type of funeral was reserved for the bravest warriors and most respected chieftains.

Wagner has even made use of the version of Balder's life recounted by Saxo Grammaticus, most notably in the episode of Siegfried's encounter with the Rhinemaidens in *Götterdämmerung* Act III. In Saxo's account Balder's rival Hother (here not Balder's brother) is in love with, and loved by, Hother's foster-sister Nanna. One day Balder, seeing Nanna and falling passionately in love with her, resolves to slay Hother. Shortly thereafter

> Hother is led astray during the hunt by a fog, and comes upon a home of forest maidens *(Waldjungfrauen)* who greet him by name. He asks them who they are. They answer that they have the power to direct the outcome of war. Often they are invisibly present at battles, and by secretly supporting their friends they decide the outcome in their favour. Thus they can distribute fortune or misfortune as they please. . . . They warn him not to attack Balder with weapons, although he deserves to be hated intensely, because he is a demigod, conceived by special divine seed. [18]

This event inspired the NL's account of Hagen's meeting with the mermaids who prophesy the Burgundians' downfall in Hunland. Wagner, however, derived his scene of Siegfried and the Rhinemaidens not from the NL but directly from the same source as the epic's: Saxo's account of Hother, which Dr. Ludwig Frauer included in his book on Valkyries. Even the original name Wagner gave the Rhinemaidens – *Wasserjungfrauen* – echoes Frauer's *Waldjungfrauen*, and significantly the Rhinemaidens' first appearance in what was to become *The Ring* was in this very scene in *Siegfrieds Tod* (later *Götterdämmerung*). The other elements too come straight from Saxo's account: the hero led astray during a hunt, the maidens greeting him by name, the warning of impending danger. [19]

Here, then, we have the Wagnerian hero in all his splendour. The two streams of influence – *myth*: the bright, shining god of peace and well-being, victor over the dragon of darkness, and *history*: the brave warrior-leaders Arminius and Civilis, challenging, and victorious over, the might of Rome – have merged into *heroic legend*: the splendid figure of Siegfried, dragon-slayer, winner of treasure and power, brave and outstanding warrior – and finally produced the Siegfried of the *Ring* tetralogy, slayer of Fafner and winner of the Nibelung hoard, heroic fighter who never turns his back on an enemy. But how far does he retain his glory and splendour? Does that glory become tarnished when he steps off his quasi-mythical pedestal into the pseudo-historical world of the Gibichungs? The answers will have to wait until Chapter Four, for in the meantime we must meet The Heroine.

## Notes

1. Translated in Cooke, p. 98.

2. Many martyr graves were found in that area in the eighth century.

3. St. Victor is often portrayed slaying a dragon.

4. *Annalen*, p. 111.

5. *ibid.*, p. 111.

6. The premiere was in 1835.

7. Hermann Kesting, *Der Befreier Arminius im Lichte der geschichtlichen Quellen und der wissenschaftlichen Forschung*, Detmold, 1962; quoted in Döbler, p. 158.

8. Mone, p. 3.

9. p. 42.

10. Mone, p. 2.

11. An obvious parallel can be drawn with the story of Moses.

12. *The Masks of God: Creative Mythology*, pp. 119f.

13. *Gods of the North*, p. 10.

14. Hel is not a place of punishment but merely that part of the underworld to which those go who have not met their deaths on the battlefield.

15. Davidson, p. 102.

16. Branston, p. 251.

17. pp. 221f.

18. Frauer, pp. 37f.

19. Moreover, some critics have suggested that Hother and Balder have changed roles in Saxo's version.

# 3

# The Heroine:

# Wisdom, Love and Rivalry

The 'Heroine' figure in *The Ring* embodies a variety of roles:

1. valkyrie or shield-maiden, participating in battle, at Wotan's behest granting victory to one combatant or another;
2. source of wisdom for the hero: after her awakening by him she imparts magic runes and good counsel to him before he sets off 'zu neuen Taten';
3. the hero's wife, won with difficulty but, once attained, faithful, even to being a mourning widow;
4. a cause of the hero's downfall, plotting his murder with Hagen in revenge for his betrayal of her.

In Wagner's tetralogy all of these roles are encompassed in one character – Brünnhilde, 'the greatest of great women'; thus a relative of Brynhild describes her to Sigurd in the VS, and thus Wagner intended his Brünnhilde to be, for it was only fitting that Siegfried, the most splendid of heroes, should have 'the greatest of great women' predestined from all time as his wife. In legend, however, these roles are shared by, or divided among, at least three different characters – including the forerunners of Gutrune, who to Wagner's Siegfried was 'never his wife, but only his mistress' – who from an historical-evolutionary viewpoint are inextricably linked.

The evolution from history of the heroines in the Siegfried legend is a highly complex process, because with the exception of the fourth role – that of participator in his murder, traceable to well-recorded persons and events in Migration-Period and Merovingian history – the roles in which the heroines appear can be traced not so much to series of specific historical personages as to customs, events and religious observances rooted in ancient Germanic tradition.

The role of *wise-woman* is an excellent illustration of this. The idea of a mediator between the Highest Authority – God – and the world of men is a nearly universal one; the revelations of the prophets in the Judaeo-Christian tradition is the example perhaps most familiar to us. Among the ancient Germans women believed to have been specially favoured by the gods played a central part in the process of the imparting of wisdom from gods to men. Tacitus records how the Germans

> believe that there resides in women an element of holiness and a
> gift of prophecy; and so they do not scorn to ask their advice, or
> lightly disregard their replies. [1]

When such a woman exercised her special gifts *only a recognised leader had direct access to her prophecies.* One particular wise-woman, indeed with significant bearing on the Siegfried legend, was a prophetess called *Veleda* (probably not her proper name but a designation, 'seeress'), whose support was vital to the Batavian revolt against Rome in 69 A.D. She made her prophecies from a tower in which she concealed herself, and apparently only Civilis, as leader, could consult her directly for her advice.

Given the chronic unrest among the various Germanic tribes, counselling and prophesying about the outcome of battles and wars would probably have emerged as the most important function to which the seeresses' duties could be channeled. It was not, however, the only way in which ancient Germanic women were associated with war, for it was not unheard-of for them actually to participate in combat. The most memorable instance of this occurred towards the end of the second century B.C. during the conflicts between the Romans and the Cimbri, occasioned by that tribe's desperate search for new land in which to settle their families.

> When it came to the crunch . . . the women inflamed their men
> with fervent entreaties not to allow them to be handed into
> Roman slavery, and to think of their children's future. They
> bandaged the wounded, tried to instill new courage in the
> wavering, and even . . . in dire necessity participated in the
> battle, prepared to perish with the men rather than survive in
> degrading servitude. [2]

The bravery of the unflinching Cimbrian women was not only
recorded by historians but also, with the tribe's survival at
stake, celebrated in legend.

The twofold role of Germanic women in connection with
war – as prophetess and participant – was combined in myth
and legend in the figure of the *valkyrie*. The word itself *valkyrja*
literally means 'female chooser of the slain', and may in its
earliest connotation reflect

> a memory . . . of the priestesses of the god of war . . . who
> officiated at the sacrificial rites when captives were put to death
> after battle . . . Since it was often decided by lot which prisoners
> should be killed, the idea that the god 'chose' his victims,
> through the instrument of the priestesses, must have been a
> familiar one . . . [3]

At any rate, the oldest conception of valkyries to have survived
in myth and legend is that of warrior maidens who rode
through the skies, carrying out the will of the war-god and
escorting selected heroes to Valhalla. As the act of *fulfilling* a
god's will could be considered to imply *making known* that will
it follows that the gift of prophecy also counted among a
valkyrie's attributes; thus the valkyries were also kin to the
Norns and other mythical manifestations of second-sighted
female beings.

Later on, valkyrie qualities became attributed as well to the
outstanding female figures of heroic legend who derived
ultimately from historical events: 'Wives of living heroes.
Human princesses are said to become Valkyries. . .' [4] Frauer [5]
offers a penetrating summary of the 'human valkyries of
heroic poetry:

The figures of the heroic sagas [as opposed to the valkyries of the poems on the gods] appear almost exclusively as humans . . . Indeed, not the pure, unadulterated human nature; [the Scandinavians] feel compelled to ensure the significance of these figures through attributing to them, at least in part, extraordinary power and might, gigantic bodily proportions, strength, courage and, accordingly, achievement of the greatest deeds; sovereignty over nature and human beings, which breaks through the usual limits of human effectiveness in many areas; astounding wisdom, especially foreknowledge of the future; . . . on the whole, magical powers of every kind. Above all the important maidens and women, whom the [heroic poetry of the] *Elder Edda* tells about, appear in this supernatural light. They participate in all the above-mentioned privileges and arts. As true Germanic wives, however, they take the most interest in war and battles. To be sure, to some extent they appear to us only as human beings; their human parents and their home are named; they marry and live with their husbands; or go into battle, as do the shield-maidens. At the same time, however, their human nature secretly changes to a superhuman one; through their participation in war, their direction of it in the name of Odin, they are no longer human females, no longer shield-maidens, but complete valkyries, differing from the former only in that they associate themselves with particular heroes in the manner of human women.

Brynhild was one such heroine, renowned especially for her soothsaying powers. In *Brot* she recounts a dream she has after Sigurd's murder, foretelling the destruction of the Giukungs, while in *Skamma*, as she lies dying, she foretells Gudrun's marriage to Atli and her reconciliation with her brothers, Gunnar's death in the snake-pit, the fearful end of Atli and his sons and the subsequent history of Gudrun and her daughter Swanhild. The VS, not unexpectedly, elaborates upon this aspect of Brynhild; for example, before Sigurd has met the Giukungs Gudrun goes to consult Brynhild, whom she has never met (therefore Brynhild must enjoy a reputation as a seeress), about the meaning of a dream she has had. Brynhild recognises Gudrun before they meet from a dream she had of her the previous night, and interprets Gudrun's dream as foretelling future events concerning Sigurd.

Nor did Gudrun lack the Valkyrie aura, in her case especially

the ancient Germanic courage in the face of battle; *Atlamál*
relates how she took up weapons to fight on her brothers' side
when they had been trapped by Atli's men:

> Preparing for battle she cast off her cloak,
> seized a sword to defend her kinsmen.
> The fighting was fierce where she wielded her weapon.
> The daughter of Giuki brought down two warriors,
> felled Atli's brother and rendered him helpless,
> aiming her blow so she struck off his foot.
> Another she smote, a mortal blow dealt him,
> despatched him to Hel; yet her hand never trembled.

The application of 'valkyrie' features to Brynhild will be
treated further in due course, but first it remains to discuss the
most important valkyrie *per se* to figure in the Siegfried legend:
Sigrdrifa, the heroine of *Sigrdrifumál*. Sigurd, continuing his
journey after having slain Fafner, happens upon a woman
sleeping on a mountain top from which a great light is shining
like a fire. He awakens her; she calls herself 'Sigrdrifa' – a term
often considered to be not a proper name but an epithet,
'victory bringer' – and explains that she is a valkyrie whom
Odin has sunk into a magic sleep as punishment for
disobedience. She then imparts magic runes and many words
of good counsel to Sigurd.

In some later works, notably the VS, a conflation of Sigrdrifa
with Brynhild has occurred, with the result that Brynhild
absorbs the role of the awakened valkyrie. Originally,
however, they were quite separate figures, having evolved
from different historical antecedents. The essential theme of
the 'awakening of Sigrdrifa' episode in its most ancient form
was to depict the *relationship between heroism and wisdom*:
just as the historical tribal leader had access to the seeress'
counsel because of his high position, so too did Sigurd, as a
consequence of his heroism in braving the flames, receive the
runes from the Valkyrie. Here history has combined with myth
to produce poetry infused with religious significance, for the
runes and counsel embodied in *Sigrdrifumál* must reflect the
precepts of the old Nordic-Germanic pagan religion.

The idea of a love-swearing between Sigurd and Sigrdrifa exists only in later prose additions to the *Edda* and in those later works which conflate the valkyrie with Brynhild, notably the *Ride to Hel* and the VS; in other words it is a relatively recent idea, and *not extant in any poem in which Sigrdrifa is a distinct entity from Brynhild:* in *Gripisspá*, for example, they are two separate persons and Sigurd's relationship with the valkyrie is strictly platonic.[6]

The wife figure, embodying themes of courtship and love, evolved quite distinctly from the wisdom-imparting valkyrie, and moreover, from an historical-evolutionary point of view she established her place in the Siegfried legend backwards, appearing first not as a bride to be won but as a wife or widow mourning the loss of her husband. The earliest historical model is Thusnelda, wife of Arminius, who after her kidnapping by the Romans never saw her husband again and bore him a son in captivity.

That Thusnelda's sad fate made a deep impression on the popular consciousness appears to be testified to by certain archaeological finds[7] that are believed to depict her. Even in the nineteenth century Thusnelda, like Arminius, inspired many art works, and ranked next to the Nibelung legend as one of the favourite subjects of painters of historical themes.[8] Thusnelda, as prototype of a sorrowing woman, grieving at the loss of her husband, survives in the Siegfried legend in the image of Kriemhild or Gudrun, who weep and mourn ceaselessly for the dead hero.

It was suggested in Chapter Two that a bride-winning adventure may have become attached to the Siegfried legend because some of the historical wives, as interesting persons in their own right, would have inspired this. Another, at least equally important impulse for a bride-winning episode must have come from the high esteem in which chastity and the marriage vows were held by the ancient Germans. Tacitus records that the Germans observed a very strict marriage code; indeed 'no feature of their morality deserves higher praise· · · No one . . . calls it "up-to-date" to seduce and be seduced.'[9] Polygamy was unheard-of except to a limited extent among rulers, and in the marriage ceremony itself the woman 'is reminded . . . that she enters her husband's home to be the partner of his toils and perils, that both in peace and in war she is to share his sufferings and adventures'.[10] Further, there endured such wedding customs as the running of a race between bride and bridegroom and the capturing of the bride, which alluded to that most ancient form of weddings, bride-kidnapping, and which symbolised the total loosening of the woman's bonds to her former family so that she was now free to enter the new – her husband's – community.[11]

Given these circumstances it is easy to see how the acquisition of a bride could in legend have taken on the proportions of a heroic act and to postulate such an episode with regard to Sigurd and Brynhild. But a postulation it must remain; circumstances surrounding Sigurd's first meeting with Brynhild are shrouded in mystery, for there is no *early* extant source with details of how they first met. The relevant section of *Brot* is missing, the action of the much later *Skamma* begins with Sigurd's arrival at Giuki's court, and the late *Ride to Hel* identifies Brynhild with Sigrdrifa. On the other hand, a heroic act, in the form of surmounting a magic fire, did occur in connection with Sigurd's wooing of Brynhild on behalf of Gunnar. This, however, leads us further on into our story than we want to go just now, for before leaving the events of Sigurd and Brynhild's early history we must discuss the conflation of Sigrdrifa and Brynhild, as this has important bearing on the sources and, in turn, on *The Ring*.

Undoubtedly the fusion of the two characters was precipitated by their sharing of certain important features. For example, as we have seen, even human, essentially historically-derived heroines tended to acquire 'valkyrie' attributes, and thus it is possible that the conflation of Sigrdrifa and Brynhild was partially triggered by the latter's possession of such valkyrie features as prophetic gifts and a hint of a bellicose nature. But even more important was the fact that only to a chosen man of heroic stature were Sigrdrifa's wisdom and counsel, and Brynhild's love and favours as a woman, available. This common quality of *inaccessibility* or, in terms of mythical motifs, Sigrdrifa's and Brynhild's embodiment of the 'maiden difficult to attain', must have been the decisive factor in the conflation of the two figures.

That the two characters have been combined, and qualities and events transferred to Brynhild which originally pertained to or involved Sigrdrifa, has produced in the VS a number of inconsistencies connected with Brynhild. One of these concerns the exercising of her powers as a seeress. Her initial dream-interpreting encounter with Gudrun shows that she has forehand knowledge of all that will come to pass; and yet later she is surprised when, during the quarrel with Gudrun, she learns the true identity of the man who rode through the flames to woo her. Moreover, she knows of the 'evil drink [Grimhild] gave Sigurd, so that he no longer remembered my name'; yet she declares to Gunnar that Sigurd has betrayed them all, as if she were unaware that the drink had caused him to forget his previous oaths. The activities of a seeress make effective reading indeed, but these additional examples of Brynhild's soothsaying powers do not concur with the references to betrayal so essential to the story.

A more serious incongruity involves the illogicality of Sigurd's various visits to Brynhild before her marriage to Gunnar. The first visit is that which in the Eddic poetry was made to Sigrdrifa. It begins with Sigurd seeing

> a great light on the fell, as if a fire were burning there, which rose toward the heavens. When he came closer a shield-castle stood there, on the top of which a banner was flying.

He then enters the castle, espies the sleeping, byrny-clad maiden and awakens her.

The second encounter – which is related as if Sigurd and Brynhild were meeting for the first time – occurs at Hlymdale, the home of Brynhild's foster-father Heimir; even within this account there occur contradictions. Heimir

> was married to Brynhild's sister, who was named Bekkhild because she had remained at home and learned handicraft, but Brynhild went clad in a helmet and a coat of mail and took part in battles, which was why she was called Brynhild.

But a few paragraphs later the author relates how Brynhild 'came home to Heimir',

> and she sat in a room with her maidens. She was more skilled in handicraft than other women. She used gold thread for her needlepoint and wove therein the great deeds which Sigurd had done . . .

This description would seem more to suit the Bekkhild of the previous page than Brynhild the shield-maiden. Sigurd then comes to Hlymdale and enters the tower in which Brynhild is sitting; the two speak, he gives her a gold ring and they renew the oaths of love sworn on the mountain.

On his third visit Sigurd is accompanied by Gunnar and Hogni; they come to claim Brynhild as Gunnar's wife. When they arrive at Hlymdale Heimir tells them he believes that Brynhild will wed only the man

> who would ride through the flaming fire that surrounded her house. They found the house and the fire and saw there a fortress with a golden roof ridge, around which burned a fire.

Why could not Sigurd have decisively claimed Brynhild as his wife on the occasion of his first visit to her fire-surrounded mountain home? If, on the other hand, one wants to take the view that the first account, describing a light shining 'like a fire' on the mountain top, does not literally imply fire surrounding the mountain top in the way that the account of the third visit does, then one still might ask why Brynhild on that first occasion swore oaths of love with a man who had not braved the wall of flames, contrary to her resolution as expressed later.

Further, when Sigurd arrives the third time, in Gunnar's guise, and they plight their troth, Brynhild is at home alone and Heimir hears only after the event about what has come to pass; yet later the version of that wooing which Brynhild relates corresponds to that in *Skamma*, namely that she was pressured by her immediate family (her father Budli or brother Atli) into marrying the man who had come riding on Grane to propose to her.

In general the difficulties stem from the failure of the author, who fashioned his account from many different sources, to exercise sufficient discretion in taking the anomalies into account and sorting out the conflicting elements which were bound to exist from source to source. The root of the problem presented by Sigurd's various visits to Brynhild is that the material from which the author fashioned the account of the second visit was incorporated from Eddic sources that originally had nothing to do with Sigurd and Brynhild and yet contained features – notably the surmounting of magic flames, the help of a magic sword and horse, and the granting of protective charms over the hero – which remarkably parallel elements in the poems on Sigrdrifa and Brynhild. These sources are *Skirnismál*, about Freyr's wooing of Gerd, and *Svipdagsmál*, about Svipdag's wooing of Menglöd. For some reason – to speculate on what it might be is outside the scope of this discussion – the saga author has decided to adapt this material into the Sigurd and Brynhild story, making it describe a second encounter between them which occurs between their first meeting (originally the hero's encounter with, and awakening of, the Valkyrie) and the one whose purpose is to propose on behalf of Gunnar.[12]

It was the blood-spattered events that transpired during the sixth century, however, which were decisive in the development of Brünnhilde into the formidable figure of legend and, along with this, the introduction of a rival female equal in stature: Gudrun or Kriemhild. Here Brünnhilde enters Gunther's world, and her initiation into that false world signals her step down from the pedestal of the mythical 'bride difficult to attain' to the historically-inspired roles of betrayed woman, of antagonist in a bloody vendetta which entails the entry of the rival woman, and of instigator of the hero's death.

The concept of *two rival women* in the Siegfried legend evolved from three historical cases of female rivalry. Moreover, the feud between them precipitates Siegfried's murder, with the introduction of a *woman as responsible for the slaying*.

From the pages of Gothic history comes the account of a strong and mighty Goth named Uraja, possessor of a great treasure, who ceded the kingship to his friend Ildibad. One day Uraja's wife insulted the wife of Ildibad. When the Queen demanded respect from her subject Uraja's wife replied, 'Don't you know that Uraja really ought to have been king, and that it is he who has made Ildibad king and you queen?'[13] The Queen, incensed, demanded that her husband avenge the insult, whereupon Ildibad caused unjust accusations to be brought against Uraja, had him murdered and took possession of his treasure. The similarities with the Siegfried legend are striking: the quarrel between the two women (*cf.* Chapter One) as to who enjoys the greater prestige (Wagner: Brünnhilde's humiliation at being given over to Gunther), the slandering and murder of one of the husbands who owns a great treasure (Wagner: the murder of Siegfried on the pretext that he had broken his oath to Gunther) and the appropriation of that treasure by his opponent (Wagner: the attempts by Gunther and Hagen to seize Siegfried's ring).

The most notorious feud to have etched a lasting place in the historical annals of that era – and which played an indispensable part in the development of the Siegfried and Nibelung legends – was that involving the sixth-century Merovingian King Sigebert and his wife, the Visigothic princess Brunechild, the most renowned of all historical models for Siegfried and Bruñnhilde. Grandson of King Clovis of the Franks, Sigebert was the son of Lothar I, upon whose death his kingdom, and his treasure, were divided among his four sons, Charibert, Guntram, Chilperich and Sigebert. Thus, despite the geographical split, the four brothers were, effectively, *co-rulers* of the Frankish kingdom.

It was through his marriage to *Brunechild* that Sigebert achieved immortality in heroic legend. Gregory of Tours relates how Sigebert

> sent messengers loaded with gifts to Spain and asked for the hand of Brunhild, the daughter of King Athanagild. This young woman was elegant in all that she did, lovely to look at, chaste and decorous in her behaviour, wise in her generation and of good address. Her father did not refuse to give her to Sigebert, but sent her off with a large dowry. [14]

Soon afterwards Sigebert's brother Chilperich asked for and received Brunechild's sister *Galswintha* in marriage. Gregory reports with some irony. 'He loved her very dearly, for she had brought a large dowry with her.'[15] However, this did not prevent Chilperich from keeping *Fredegunde*, a woman to whom he had been married before he wed Galswintha.[16] Galswintha had to endure many insults from Fredegunde; she complained about it to Chilperich, even begging to be allowed to return home. At last Chilperich had Galswintha murdered, presumably at Fredegunde's instigation.

As a result of Fredegunde's part in this deed Brunechild swore a blood feud with her sister-in-law, a feud which prolonged and intensified the fraternal strife and civil wars to which the contentious Merovingians were anyhow prone. During one such campaign between Sigebert and Chilperich Sigebert himself was murdered by two assassins sent by Fredegunde who stabbed him with poisoned knives, a deed which still further exacerbated the vendetta between the two women.

The quarrel between the Gothic wives of Uraja and Ildibad gave rise in legend to a purely political quarrel between the women as exemplified in the NL,[17] while the complicated Merovingian events, above all the protracted feud between Brunechild and Fredegunde, reinforced the political rivalry but also, through the Fredegunde-Galswintha-Chilperich episode, introduced a personal feud which in both history and in legend pivots around the Fredegunde/Gudrun figure: in history we have the Fredegunde-Galswintha rivalry and in the saga the Gudrun-Brynhild rivalry. Consistent in both Frankish history and in legend is the role of the sister-in-law (Fredegunde in history, Brynhild in Nordic legend) as instigator of Siegfried's murder.

The feud – the prestige conflict in which she becomes embroiled with her sister-in-law – is the central event of the heroine's later life. The exact nature of this conflict differs from source to source but is instigated by a discussion between the two women of the relative merits of their respective husbands. Brynhild's jealousy in the *Edda* is the germ of the conflict, yet in only one poem is an actual quarrel hinted at: in the *Ride to Hel* which, it is worth remembering, is a late poem. Brynhild tells the Giantess:

> Gudrun, daughter of Giuki, reproached me
> that I had slept in Sigurd's arms;
> then did I know what I rather had not,
> that I was betrayed, the wrong man's bride.

This passage must have either been the basis for the more developed quarrel in the VS, or itself have been based on a lost poem (such as the missing section of *Brot*) which in turn provided the basis for the VS quarrel. In the saga the prestige question first concerns whose husband has greater preeminence, and then proceeds to which of the two women has the greater claim to be Sigurd's spouse: consequently the figure of Gudrun is more substantial than in the corresponding sections of the *Edda*. Brynhild had sworn an oath to marry only the man heroic enough to brave the wall of flame surrounding her dwelling. When Sigurd, disguised as Gunnar, achieves this, she agrees to marry Gunnar, although she is puzzled because she had expected it to be Sigurd, who had awakened her and with whom she had plighted her troth, who would ride the flames. Later, however, she and Gudrun fall to quarrelling over whose husband was the most splendid hero, and Gudrun, who, like Grimhild her mother, was aware of Sigurd and

Brynhild's previous relationship, reveals to the latter that it was not Gunnar but Sigurd who rode through the fire to court her; as proof she exhibits the ring which Brynhild had given Sigurd during the three nights he lived with her on the mountain in Gunnar's guise, and which he in turn had passed on to Gudrun. While the jealousy motive of the *Edda* remains – Brynhild declares to Gudrun, 'You shall pay for the fact that Sigurd is your man; I resent that you delight in him and enjoy his great wealth' – the dominant emotion for Brynhild is anger over the broken oaths: Sigurd has broken his own oaths to Brynhild and has caused her to break her oath to wed only the hero who knows no fear and who rides the fire.

The VS is alone among the three epics to have the quarrel continue to the question of who has the greater claim on Sigurd; in the case of the NL this would be impossible anyway, as the South German epic knows of no love relationship between Siegfried and Brunhild. Thus the prestige question in the NL and Ths., particularly the former, is more political than personal, hinging on the status of the two husbands.

In the NL, when Siegfried and Gunther journeyed to Iceland to win Brunhild as the latter's wife, they pretended that Siegfried was Gunther's vassal in order to make Gunther seem the eminent king, a worthy prospective husband for Brunhild. Consequently Brunhild has continued to think this to be the case during all the time she has been married to Gunther. One day, after the two couples have been married for ten years, Brunhild and Kriemhild begin discussing and comparing the merits of their respective husbands: Brunhild of course believes Gunther to be the nobler man, while Kriemhild in her turn denies Gunther's superiority and, unaware of Siegfried's pretence of vassalage in Iceland, is offended by the implication that her brothers should have married her off to a liegeman. The quarrel comes to a head later the same day, when the two ladies and their entourages are about to enter the Cathedral for vespers. Brunhild orders Kriemhild to halt with the words, 'A liegewoman may not enter before a Queen!' To this Kriemhild retorts, 'How could a vassal's paramour ever wed a King?'[18] When Brunhild demands an explanation of this remark Kriemhild reveals that Siegfried, and not Gunther, overpowered Brunhild and took her virginity.[19] The Ths. version runs parallel to this, the quarrel being instigated by Grimhild's failure to rise when Brynhild, Queen of the land, enters the hall and culminating in Grimhild's revelation that it was not Gunnar but Sigurd who was Brynhild's first man.

Regardless of the exact nature of each quarrel, common to all three works is the function of the quarrel as the occasion on which the hero's alleged transgressions are revealed, which ultimately results in his murder for revenge.

Through the Gothic and Merovingian feuds *vengeance-seeking* entered the legend. As Ildibad's wife sought retribution for her humiliation at the hands of Uraja's wife and Galswintha demanded an end to Fredegunde's insults, so did Brunhild in the NL crave vengeance for Kriemhild's public declaration that Siegfried had made her, Brunhild, his paramour, and in the Ths. for Sigurd's humiliation of her in having taken her virginity and told his wife about it. As the formidable Queen Brunechild pursued to its limits the bloody feud with her sister-in-law in revenge for the *assassination of her husband*, so did Kriemhild do the same to her brothers for the murder of Siegfried. Finally, just as Brunechild sought to avenge the *murder of her sister* Galswintha, so too in legend did Gudrun seek vengeance on Atli for the murders of her brothers Gunnar and Hogni; additionally, the historical sister-vengeance survives in Atli's murder of the Giukungs allegedly in retribution for the death of his sister Brynhild, which we have already seen to be a later addition to rather than an original element in the legend. In the North the sibling-vengeance essentially supplants the husband-vengeance: in conformity with the North's unfavourable picture of Atli Gudrun's potential desire for avenging her husband's death is eliminated through her drinking of the potion that obliterates her memory of her brothers' slaying of Sigurd, thus letting Atli's greed for the treasure become the reason for the downfall of her kin. Further, the legend added a new, personal vengeance motive to an historico-political occurrence: Fredegunde, accomplishing the assassination of Sigebert in the context of civil war, becomes in legend Brynhild demanding Sigurd's life in order to avenge (in the North) the deception by which she was made to marry Gunnar, or (on the Continent) the humiliation of Siegfried's boasting that he had taken her virginity.

Thus has Queen Brunechild been immortalised as a valkyrie-like figure – a noble lady deciding between victor and vanquished in a battle: what concept could more appropriately be associated with Queen Brunechild who, by her own nephew Lothar's accusation – echoed in the Giantess' grim salutation in the *Ride to Hel*:

> You have, fair woman, if you want to know,
> washed from your hands the blood of heroes . . .
> Born to cause the world's worst misfortune
> were you, Brynhild, daughter of Budli!

– brought about the deaths of no less than ten Frankish princes through her bloody feud with Fredegunde? And so Thusnelda, passively grieving for the loss of her husband, becomes the wife actively seeking vengeance for this loss: Brynhild, demanding the death of her brother-in-law (Sigurd) for deceiving her into marrying someone other than himself whom she should have married, and Kriemhild, precipitating the downfall of her kin (the Burgundians) to avenge their slaying of her husband.

Yet nor is Brynhild, that complex personality, without her softer, more sympathetic side: for in Galswintha, imported from Visigothic Spain to the Frankish kingdom ostensibly to become Chilperich's wife,· only to find herself a pawn in a prestige game between Chilperich and Sigebert and compelled to yield precedence to her husband's chief wife/mistress Fredegunde, we have the *betrayed woman* of legend: Brynhild in the VS, cruelly tricked into marrying a man incapable of

fulfilling the conditions stipulated by her instead of the fearless
hero whom alone she swore she would marry; in *Skamma* and
the VS, yearning to return home to her kin rather than
continue to live among her betrayers: indeed the strong
historical influence in the moulding of *Skamma* is quite
obvious, for the idea of an arranged royal marriage combined
with the threat of disinheritance – Atli vows to deprive
Brynhild of her birthright if she will not accept Gunnar's
marriage proposal – certainly smacks of political intrigue. The
fate of Galswintha, assumed into the figure of Brynhild, left the
door open for Brunechild, the historical wife of Sigebert, to
become Brynhild, the would-be but betrayed wife.

It is obvious – indeed, it was inevitable – that *no direct
one-to-one correspondence exists between an historical
Merovingian woman and a legendary 'counterpart'*: instead,
extensive transference of characteristics took place between
the historical Brunechild, Fredegunde and Galswintha on one
hand and the legendary Brunhild/Brynhild and Gudrun/
Kriemhild on the other. As one commentator explains:[20]

> Whoever in the sixth or seventh centuries spoke of Brunhild
> thought also of her antagonist Fredegunde and the blood feud
> that life ordained for them. The deadly hostility of the queens
> also occupied the singers, who took the material for their lays
> from the present or the recent past.

Important to those who gave the earliest expression to the
legend was not a faithful reproduction of the individual details
of a life from an historical to a legendary figure, but *the general
idea of two extraordinarily powerful women inexorably locked
in a bloody feud* whose consequences reached far beyond the
spheres of their own immediate lives:

> The Merovingian ruler [Brunechild] was such an incomparable
> figure that she must have been an ideal subject for the court
> singers. She was predestined for the unreal, fabulous figure of
> poetry.
> [ And when one reads these lines in the NL:
> . . . through the feuding of two women
> was many a hero lost
> the verse can refer equally to Brunhild and Kriemhild and to the
> queens Brunhild and Fredegunde. [21]

One aspect of the historical Brunechild not reflected in legend is her terrible death: having been arraigned before her nephew Lothar, the son of Fredegunde, and condemned for the death of ten Merovingian kings,

> she was tortured for three days; then, tied by the hair, one arm and one leg to a wild horse, she was dragged across rough ground until she died. [22]

In the NL Brunhild merely fades from the story after the Burgundians set out for Etzel's kingdom, a fitting end (in the poet's eyes, that is, and perhaps those of his audience) for a character who, as an unavoidable reminder of a more primitive, heathen era, constituted something of an embarrassment to the refined, mediaeval Christian audience. In the Ths. Queen Brynhild survives all the main characters. At the end, after Aldrian – Hogni's son and Brynhild's nephew – has encompassed Attila's death by shutting him into the mountain containing Sigurd's treasure, she gives him an army with which to take possession of Niflungenland: surely a reflection of Brunechild, who acted as regent for two under-aged Merovingian monarchs, her five-year-old son Childebert II after Sigebert's assassination, and many years later her great-grandson Sigebert II, whom she herself named king upon the death of the boy's father Theuderich.

Only the Nordic tradition as exemplified in the *Edda* and the VS actually depicts Brynhild's death, and there we are not disappointed, for it is a dramatic one indeed. After the slaying of Sigurd Brynhild stabs herself and, at her own request, is burned alongside him on the funeral pyre. This manner of death was inspired by the custom of suttee, by which a widow was killed or committed suicide and her body burned on her husband's funeral pyre.

The scholar H.R. Ellis Davidson mentions a passage in the *Flateyjarbok*, a book of sagas of the Norwegian kings, which 'implies that the custom of suttee was practised in Sweden in honour of Odin until the tenth century'.[23] Further, reports

58

Dr. Davidson,

> There are so many references either to a deliberate act of
> suicide by a widow or to a sudden death 'of grief 'at the funeral in
> the literary sources, that some vague memory of the custom of
> sacrifice of the wife at her husband's funeral seems to have
> survived from heathen times.

The association of this custom with the heathen North has given rise to the assumption that the circumstances of Brynhild's death in the *Edda* are a Scandinavian accretion on the legend. While this is highly possible it cannot be taken for granted, for suttee was also practised among some Continental German tribes, notably the Heruli;[24] in fact it could be from this tribe that the custom reached the North, for in the sixth century the Heruli, originally a tribe from southern Sweden who migrated to the Continent and lived there for several centuries,

> turned about-face – having been forcibly persuaded to do so by
> the Langobards – and made their way back to Scandinavian
> parts, no doubt carrying with them much of what they had
> learned on their travels.[25]

Thus it is even conceivable that suttee – or the widow's 'sudden death "of grief" ' – existed in an early version of the Siegfried legend which featured the 'sorrowing wife' figure. At any rate, Brynhild's death on Sigurd's funeral pyre substantiates her claim as the original wife figure of the legend and that the *Edda*, and particularly the poem we know as *Brot*, must have contained some idea of her having been his intended bride.

Until now we have said very little about the NL Brunhild. The reason is that, as with the NL Siegfried, there was little material of use for Wagner's 'greatest of great women'. As we have seen the poet drastically minimises any aspects of the characters which smack of heathenism, which includes eschewing his ancestors' ·reverence for prophetesses and warrior women: when the mediaeval Siegfried, Gunther and their noble knights die it is the Christian heaven to which they go; not for them the valkyrie's summons to Valhalla. Accordingly Brunhild is an ordinary mortal woman whose extraordinary powers have degenerated into purely physical, Amazonian strength. The poet first describes her as being

> of vast strength and surpassing beauty. With her love as the prize, she vied with brave warriors at throwing the javelin, and the noble lady also hurled the weight to a great distance and followed with a long leap; and whosoever aspired to her love had, without fail, to win these three tests against her, or else, if he lost but one, he forfeited his head. [26]

A more detailed description of her physical prowess appears in the account of how Siegfried won Brunhild for Gunther – a sort of Olympics in miniature – and her strength comes into play again during her farcical wedding night with Gunther:

> [Gunther] tried to win her by force, and tumbled her shift for her, at which the haughty girl reached for the girdle of stout silk cord that she wore round about her waist, and . . . bound him head and foot, carried him to a nail, and hung him on the wall . . . He had to stay hanging there the whole night through till dawn, when the bright morning shone through the windows. [27]

Consequently Wagner modelled his Brünnhilde essentially on her Nordic forbears. To start with, he accepted the identification of Brynhild and Sigrdrifa; however, his combination of these two figures is so brilliantly successful that merely to credit him with accepting the VS' conflation would be a gross understatement; in fact, it is fair to suggest that had the conflation not existed in any of the sources, Wagner would have conceived it anyway, for he had reasons consistent with his own interpretation of the source material for fusing the two characters. Wagner's identification of Brünnhilde with the Valkyrie serves to retain the connection between heroism and wisdom enshrined in the story of the awakening of Sigrdrifa, and it fulfills the important dramatic function of providing a link between the divine and the human worlds of *The Ring*. Thus Brünnhilde's life prior to Siegfried's claiming of her for Gunther incorporates events in the life of Sigrdrifa related in *Sigrdrifumál* and in those sources which fuse Brynhild with Sigrdrifa. *Die Walküre* is basically an augmentation and dramatisation of the mythico-legendary events leading up to the Valkyrie's disobedience of the war-god. The important

scene in which Brünnhilde announces to Siegmund that he is to
die – rightly described by Deryck Cooke[28] as 'really the decisive
[moment] in the whole of *The Ring* – could have been inspired
by another source than the actual poetry: Ludwig Frauer's
book. Frauer comments on the 'Valkyries' Song' in the great
thirteenth-century Icelandic prose *Nialssaga*, which song,
foretelling a terrible, bloody battle, was inspired by the Battle
of Clontarf that took place around 1014:

> It is noteworthy that the Valkyries here are also announcing the
> deaths [of King Brian and Earl Sigurd] and the outcome while
> they determine them. Both ideas concur approximately with
> pagan views; announcing is an act of decision, and the decision is
> made in the form of an announcement. [29]

From here Wagner could have derived the idea of Brünnhilde
actually announcing to Siegmund that he is doomed to die in
the forthcoming battle with Hunding. Such a confrontation
between valkyrie and warrior could thus allow Siegmund to
reject beforehand the fate destined for him, and thereby allow
Brünnhilde – because the ironic difference between her and
the valkyries of *Nialssaga* is that she does not only not
determine the fate but indeed goes against her own feelings in
having to withhold her protection from Siegmund – to give in to
him, thereby, like Sigrdrifa, disobeying Wotan and earning her
punishment.

Regarding Brünnhilde's punishment Wagner compromises
between The *Ride to Hel*, in which Odin rules that only the
bearer of Fafner's gold should ride over the fire surrounding
Brynhild's hall, and the VS, in which Brynhild herself vows
never to wed a man who knows fear, by letting Brünnhilde
conceive the idea that she should be given in marriage only to
the bravest of heroes and persuade Wotan to make this a
decree.

The conversations between Siegfried and Brünnhilde on the
mountain in *Siegfried* Act III and the *Götterdämmerung*
prologue are taken partially from the heroic colloquy of
Sigurd's first meeting with Brynhild in the VS, which in turn

derives from *Sigrdrifumál*. From the latter poem come Brünnhilde's first words upon being awakened:

| SIGRDRIFUMÁL | SIEGFRIED |
|---|---|
| Long have I slept, | Hail, O sun! |
| long have I slumbered, | Hail, O light! |
| long last the sorrows of men; | Hail, O radiant day! |
| Odin has decreed | Long was my sleep. |
| that I must remain powerless | I have been wakened: |
| over the runes of sleep | who is the hero who |
| | awoke me? |
| Hail to the Day! | Hail, O gods! |
| Hail to the sons of Day! | Hail, O world! |
| Hail to the Night and to | Hail, O shining earth! |
| Night's sister! | My sleep is over now. |
| Look upon us | I am awake, I can see: |
| with gentle eyes | it is Siegfried |
| and grant victory to us | who has awakened me. |
| who sit here! | |

Brünnhilde, like Brynhild of the saga, reveals that she has been expecting Siegfried. Her imparting of runes and counsel to the hero, to which so many lines are devoted in the *Edda* and the saga, is preserved by Wagner but not actually dramatised; it presumably took place at some time between the end of *Siegfried* and the beginning of *Götterdämmerung*, for Brünnhilde refers to it in the prologue of the latter:

What the gods told me
I have given you:
holy runes in great number . . .

Thus in this scene the wise-woman whose knowledge is reserved for the hero is linked with the chaste ideal of Germanic womanhood whose love is attained with difficulty; for the lengthy scene at the end of *Siegfried* in which the hero strives to overcome Brünnhilde's initial reluctance to submit to him could well have been inspired by Frauer, who, after pointing out that the Magic Fire of the Siegfried legend constitutes an obstacle, analyses the historical circumstances that would have led to the attainment of Brünnhilde's love being regarded as 'essentially a struggle':

> In an attitude of defiant chastity the Germanic wife does not surrender her love voluntarily; it must be wrested from her in a heated struggle of strength against strength; having arrived at the concept that even love appears to the Germans as a contest of two opposing powers, as war, we feel tempted to regard Brünnhilde's Magic Fire, over which only the bravest man can prevail, as a reflection of the bellicose, defiant attitude with which the virgin surrounds her virginity and only lets it be snatched away from her if compelled by a superior power. [30]

The inconsistencies of which the saga author was guilty in his conflation of Sigrdrifa and Brynhild were successfully avoided by Wagner. He eliminated the problem of Sigurd's several visits to Brynhild, first of all by placing Brünnhilde's resolution to wed only the hero who braves the flames well before she ever meets Siegfried, and secondly by allowing Siegfried two clear-cut visits to her, both on the same mountain-top home: the first when he awakens her and they swear vows of love and marriage, and the second when, disguised as Gunther, he goes to woo her as Gunther's wife. Moreover, he solved the dilemma caused by Brynhild's soothsaying powers – the fact that she holds Sigurd guilty of betrayal despite her knowledge of Grimhild's drink of forgetfulness – by causing Brünnhilde to lose her special valkyrie's powers as a consequence of submitting to Siegfried. Here he has recourse to the ancient belief that virginity conferred magical power or superior strength, a belief echoed in the NL, where her amazing strength deserts her once she has been subdued. Thus Brünnhilde is unaware of Hagen's drink of forgetfulness until she learns the whole truth from the Rhinemaidens after Siegfried is dead. That she knows already in Act II of *Götterdämmerung* that it was Siegfried and not Gunther who braved the magic fire the second time was due not to special powers but to her having recognised Siegfried's eyes through the Tarnhelm's disguise:

> Ha! It was he who snatched the ring from me:
> Siegfried, the traitorous thief!

[And later to Hagen:]
One single glance from his flashing eyes
– which shone brilliantly at me
even through the deceitful disguise –
would turn your highest courage to fear!

Through his successful fusion of the mythico-religious valkyrie with the historically-rooted Brynhild into his Heroine figure, and her awakening by the grandson of Wotan, Wagner solved a major problem of his tetralogy, that of achieving a smooth transition from the realm of the gods to the world of humans. But another important function of his conflation of the two figures was to allow Wagner to exploit what he believed to be the mythical significance of the hero's winning of a bride *predestined for him from time immemorial*. Regarding this predestination Wagner wrote:

> The full equality [ of the mythological relationship of Tristan to Isolde and of Siegfried to Brünnhilde ] consists in the fact that both Tristan and Siegfried, under the coercion of an illusion that makes this deed of theirs an unfree one, propose marriage on behalf of another man to a woman who has been fore-ordained by primeval law as his own wife, and meet their downfalls as a result of the incongruities arising from this deed. [31]

It is not surprising that Wagner's reading of the Eddic poems on Sigurd convinced him that he had penetrated to the *Ur-myth* of Brünnhilde's predestination as Siegfried's wife;[32] in these poems Brynhild and not Gudrun is the great heroine, and moreover, the predestination idea is often explicit. In the *Ride to Hel* Odin, in putting Brynhild to sleep as a punishment for disobedience, rules that only the man who knew no fear and who would ride over the flames with Fafner's gold can awaken her.

> On Grane came the gold's good ruler riding
> to the estate my foster-father governed.

As Brynhild relates this to the Giantess, noteworthy is the complete absence of any surprise on Brynhild's part, as if just Sigurd (the 'gold's good ruler') and no one else had been expected all along. In the VS, too, the sense of predestiny survives: Brynhild, upon her awakening, exclaims, 'Ah, it is so, that here is come Sigurd Sigmundson, bearing Fafnir's helm on his head and Fafnir's bane in his hand?'[33] Thus she immediately recognises Sigurd as the hero she had vowed to marry before she had sunk into her sleep of punishment, the man who knew no fear. Wagner's intuition about the antiquity of this idea would appear to be confirmed by its role in *Svipdagsmál* which, like its close relation *Skirnismál*, is regarded as a survival from an ancient fertility ritual: there Svipdag is acknowledged as the mate destined for Menglöd:

> There is no man intended to sleep
> in Menglöd's delightful embrace,
> except for Svipdag: the sun-bright maid
> is destined to be his bride.

In *The Ring* the concept of predestination is expressed through Wotan's decree that only the hero brave enough to ride through the magic fire can win his daughter as a wife, while both he and Brünnhilde know, without explicitly saying so, that the only hero who can do this will be Siegfried. The further implications – the 'incongruities arising' from Siegfried's contravening of this destiny – will be discussed in the next chapter.

Completely consistent with Wagner's conviction of Brünnhilde's destiny as Siegfried's wife is his diminishing of the significance of the Brünnhilde-Gutrune rivalry. This amounts to a very important deviation from all the sources because the quarrel, which plays such a central role in the epics, is reduced in *The Ring* to the brief dialogue between Brünnhilde and Gutrune towards the close of *Götterdämmerung*, after Brünnhilde enters the hall to which Siegfried's body has been borne:

> Gutrune:  Brünnhilde! Angered by jealousy!
> You brought us this tragedy,
> you stirred the men up against him.
> Woe that you ever came near this house!

| Brünnhilde: | Silence, miserable woman!<br>You were never his true wife;<br>as his mistress you were bound to him.<br>I am his real wife<br>to whom Siegfried swore eternal oaths<br>before he ever saw you. |
|---|---|
| Gutrune: | Accursed Hagen!<br>You made me give him the potion<br>that took her husband away!<br>O misery! Suddenly, now I realise:<br>Brünnhilde was the beloved<br>whom the drink made him forget! |

The idea of any jealousy on Brünnhilde's part is also minimised, the only hint of it occurring in Act II when Gunther balks at murdering Siegfried because of what it would do to Gutrune. To this Brünnhilde replies:

In helpless misery I clearly see
that Gutrune was the magic
that snatched my husband from me.
May dread strike her!

Wagner must have considered that an exaggerated display of jealousy would have been beneath his 'great woman' and reduced her to a more ordinary sort. Indeed, to have given any aspect of the Brünnhilde-Gutrune conflict greater prominence would have required Gutrune to be on a par with Brünnhilde, and for this there was no room in Wagner's tetralogy. To be sure, he could not eliminate the second woman completely, for without her the marital intrigues which eventually precipitated the downfall both of Siegfried and, ultimately, of the Gibichung dynasty could not have taken place; when Brünnhilde steps off her valkyrian pedestal into Gunther's domains, she steps into a world of which Gutrune is an integral part. And so Wagner 'demoted' Gutrune from actually being Siegfried's legitimate wife – which her literary predecessors are – to being deluded by Hagen into believing she is his wife; such a reduction of Gutrune to a mere pawn in Hagen's plot accords with the latter's role as manipulator of the intrigue as well as with Wagner's 'one true wife' concept. Wagner's reaching back beyond the sources to renew the original concept of only one woman in Siegfried's life represents a major instance of his *use of an early form of the legend no longer extant in literature.*

Although Wagner's Brünnhilde stems chiefly from the Scandinavian sources, there is one significant feature of the Nordic Brynhild from which Wagner deviates: her role as sole instigator of Sigurd's murder. In the NL Brunhild has been ousted in favour of Hagen as instigator of the deed. Wagner follows this general course, though with far greater psychological subtlety than in the more clear-cut epic. The *Ring* Hagen realises that the success of his plan requires Brünnhilde's consent and assistance (the latter in the form of information about Siegfried's vulnerable spot); thus he must stir up a situation which will drive Brünnhilde to crave revenge, and indeed, when this happens he is quick to take advantage of her enraged reaction to the events he has manipulated. The conversation between Brünnhilde and Hagen after they and Gunther are left alone in Act II is a dramatisation of the episode in the NL in which Brunhild's vengeful thoughts materialise in Hagen's resolution that Siegfried shall pay with his life for his insult to Brunhild's honour:

## NL

[Brunhild stood before the minster thinking:] 'Kriemhild must tell me more about this thing of which she accuses me so loudly, [34] sharp-tongued woman that she is. If Siegfried has boasted of it, it will cost him his life!'

[Kriemhild appears, displaying Brunhild's ring and girdle as proof of her accusations. Gunther, Siegfried and their knights appear and hear the accusations and Siegfried expresses his willingness to swear an oath to rebut them. Both men decide to forbid their wives to indulge in this kind of talk.]

Then Hagen of Troneck came to his liege lady, and, finding her in tears, asked her what was vexing her. She told him what had happened, and he at once vowed that Kriemhild's man should pay for it, else Hagen, because of that insult, would never be happy again.

[ . . Hagen said:] 'His boast that he enjoyed my dear lady shall cost him his life, or I shall die avenging it!' [35]

WAGNER

| | |
|---|---|
| Brünnhilde<br>(to herself): | What demonic cunning lies hidden here?<br>What magical plan stirred this up?<br>Where now is my knowledge which can sort<br>  out this confusion?<br>Where are my runes against this riddle?<br>O misery! Misery! Woe, yes, woe! . . .<br>Now who will offer me the sword<br>with which to cut these bonds? |
| Hagen: | Trust me, betrayed woman!<br>Whoever betrayed you, I will avenge it. |
| Brünnhilde: | On whom? |
| Hagen | On Siegfried, who betrayed you. |

Thus Brünnhilde becomes the unwitting conspirator in Hagen's plot and joins him in urging Gunther to agree to the murder. Here Wagner was able to make effective use of the drama inherent in the Nordic Brynhild's egging of Gunnar towards the slaying:

He betrayed you, and you all betrayed me!
Were I to have compensation
all the blood in the world would not expiate your guilt!
But the death of this one man
will suffice for all:
Siegfried must fall to expiate himself and you!
*(Götterdämmerung*, Act II)

Finally, Brünnhilde returns to the emulation of her Nordic forbears | through her | immolation on Siegfried's funeral pyre. Having passed from the mythico-religious 'valkyrie' state to that of the predominantly historical human woman, she now assumes a role which in the sources emerged from a fusion of history and religion, based as it is upon the historical tradition of the immolation of a woman on her husband's funeral pyre in accordance with the belief in an afterlife in which the man would require those people and possessions most important to him on this earth. But Wagner, as always, transcends the original context of his sources; for Brünnhilde's immolation represents not an ossified religious ritual but the act of redemption by which she completes the mission of returning the ring to its rightful owners and encompassing the end of the old order, of Wotan and the Teutonic gods.

Curiously enough Wagner took the material for the opening of the Immolation Scene, in which Brünnhilde commands logs to be piled up for Siegfried's funeral pyre, from a different Eddic context, *Gudrunarhvöt (The Whetting of Gudrun)*, a poem about the end of Gudrun's life. In order to avenge the death of her daughter Swanhild she exhorts her sons by her third husband, King Jonakr, to murder King Jormunrek, Swanhild's husband who was responsible for her death. After recounting her adventure-filled life for her sons in an often bitter but always moving monologue, she bids them gather logs for her funeral pyre, for she imagines that Sigurd is coming to be reunited with her:

> Bridle, O Sigurd, the black horse,
> let the swift steed hasten here!
> . . . . .
>
> Remember, Sigurd, what we declared
> when on the bed we both sat –
> that you would come from Hel to meet me,
> O hero, and I from earth to meet you?
>
> Pile up, O earls, a pyre of oakwood,
> raise it up high under heaven's vault!
> Let the fire burn a breast laden with misery,
> and melt the heavy snows in my heart!

The stanzas about Sigurd are particularly reminiscent of Wagner's early versions of the close of *Götterdämmerung* (or *Siegfrieds Tod* as it was originally called) in which he envisioned Siegfried and Brünnhilde being triumphantly and gloriously reunited in Valhalla, while the last stanza anticipates the opening lines of the Immolation Scene:

> Stout logs pile up for me
> on the bank of the Rhine!
> High and brightly let the fire blaze
> to consume the noble body of the majestic hero.

Basically, however, Wagner draws upon the spirit and drama of Brynhild's final moments for this scene. Like her Scandinavian counterpart Brünnhilde eulogises Siegfried's loyalty, and like her she appears in the role of a wise woman; only now, at the culmination of her life on earth Brünnhilde surpasses both the Eddic prophetess and her own former valkyrie nature in that her present wisdom is not a gift she was born with but a quality gained through experience.

> The purest of men had to betray me
> that a wife might gain wisdom!

In Brünnhilde that betrayal generated not jealousy or bitterness but understanding; in Wagner's eyes this must have been the justification for the epithet 'greatest of great women'.

## Notes

1. *Germania*, p. 108.

2. Nack, p. 77.

3. Davidson, p. 62.

4. *ibid.*, p. 61.

5. pp. 52f.

6. Indeed, by reason of the similarity between their names I would venture the bold suggestion that there must have been an early form of the legend in which a brother-sister relationship existed between Sigurd and Sigrdrifa, much the same as between Wagner's Brünnhilde and Siegmund in *Die Walküre*.

7. Jung, pp. 225ff.

8. Nack, p. 266.

9. *Germania*, pp. 116, 117.

10. *ibid.*, p. 117.

11. Nack, p. 75.

12. Frauer (p. 75) reports that both Müller and Grimm consider the account of the second visit to be an interpolation.

13. Berndt, p. 90.

14. p. 221.

15. p. 222.

16. Apparently the practice of polygamy died hard among the Merovingian kings.

17. *i.e.* up to the point where Kriemhild reveals the supposed truth about Brunhild's first man, where it becomes more personal.

18. pp. 113f.

19. We will see later that the poet is intentionally obscure as to whether or not this actually occurred, but it is irrelevant here. It is interesting that the NL does not parallel the VS to the extent of allowing the deceit in Iceland, in which Siegfried invisibly competed in the contests while Gunther only went through the motions, to be revealed.

20. Berndt, p. 81.

21. *ibid.*, p. 82.

22. Lasko, p. 65.

23. p. 151.

24. Döbler, p. 308.

25. Branston, p. 10.

26. p. 53.

27. p. 88. In the Ths. Brynhild's powers are mere remnants of their origins: upon Sigurd's arrival at her castle she recognises him despite having never seen him before, and on the wedding night she overcomes Gunnar so that Sigurd must be called in to subdue her.

28. p. 336.

29. p. 15.

30. pp. 82f.

31. 'Epilogischer Bericht.'

32. *Cf.* Cooke, pp. 98f.   As Cooke points out, what Wagner uncovered in the Nordic sources was not the pure, original myth but the Scandinavian superstructure.

33. pp. 221f.

34. *i.e.* that Siegfried was Brunhild's first man.

35. pp. 114ff.

4

# The Hero's Downfall

As with Brünnhilde, so with Siegfried does the transition from the heroic world of his youth to the false, manipulative world of Gunther's family parallel the transition from mythical to historico-legendary predominance in the development of his story. The central event, and indeed the most complex question of Siegfried's life following that transition, is that of his betrayal and subsequent murder. In the *Ring Cycle* Siegfried is unwittingly led into a situation that makes him appear to commit an ignoble act requiring vengeance: he is accused of breaking his blood-brotherhood oath to Gunther by making love to Brünnhilde while wooing her as a wife for him, and murdered in revenge.

The early 'Siegfried' legend was free of the complexities of the later versions (including Wagner's) surrounding the circumstances of the hero's supposed guilt and subsequent murder; it was probably first when the Siegfried story became influenced by the Burgundian legend – and above all by Frankish history – that the complications arose: brotherhood oaths sworn and broken, the jealousy of forsaken women, envy and greed for wealth and power.

Frankish history was plagued by continual strife among the Merovingian brother-kings caused by the division of the realm upon the father's death. The object of this fraternal rivalry was twofold: first of all the increased power to be gained from the appropriation of one's brother's share of the kingdom, and second, and no less important, the insurance of wealth that accompanied sovereignty, for with each Merovingian kingdom went a sizable treasure. Through using this wealth for such purposes as bestowing gifts, helping the needy and endowing churches the Merovingians upheld their power; thus what one historian[1] calls the 'treasure-hunt motive' was the principal reason for Merovingian military campaigning, for waging battles against foreign nations as well as attempting to confiscate one another's treasures.

Circumstances of the hero's downfall in the legend as we now possess it have their roots in such unstable conditions as these. The story of Arminius, slain by his in-laws because he supposedly aspired to higher power, was given further impetus through the life of the Frankish king Sigebert, whose *sharing with his brothers in the sovereignty* of the kingdom and the treasure inherited from his father led often to strife, and who met his death as a consequence of a feud whose ultimate cause was the *arranged marriages* between himself and Brunechild, and his brother Chilperich and Brunechild's sister Galswintha; nor must we forget the Goth Uraja, slain as the result of a quarrel between his wife and the wife of the man to whom he had ceded his sovereignty. These elements – power rivalry, marriage bargains, prestige quarrels between women – are the threads that run continuously through the legend of Siegfried's betrayal and death.

In the literary sources the hero's downfall stems ultimately from the fact that he has wooed and won Brynhild/Brunhild for another man, and in that act *a measure of deceit* was involved.

The idea of a man proposing to a woman on behalf of another man is not uncommon in legend or myth, and again we must look to the Eddic poem *Skírnismál*, for there it is *not Freyr himself but his servant Skirnir who proposes to Gerd on Freyr's behalf*. The influence of this myth probably dates far back in the Siegfried legend; the fact that a disguised (or rather, invisible) suitor figures in the NL certainly suggests its appearance in the legend prior to the division into separate

South German and Nordic traditions. However, in *Skirnismál* no deceit or disguise is involved: Skirnir approaches Gerd openly as himself, Freyr's ambassador. It must have been through the combined stimulus of the Freyr myth and the Chilperich-Galswintha affair that the Siegfried legend assumed its present form: from the myth came the idea of Siegfried's proposing on Gunther's behalf, while through the Merovingian story deceit entered the picture – the proposal is undertaken under false pretences.

In the sources the question of Siegfried's guilt and the reasons for his death are of a complexity foreshadowing that of *The Ring*. Following is a bare outline of the common plot; the details vary from source to source:

1. Siegfried marries Gunther's sister and woos Brunhild for Gunther.
2. A prestige argument ensues between the two wives during which Siegfried's wife reveals something concerning the circumstances of his wooing of Brunhild, which profoundly upsets the latter.
3. Brunhild consequently decides that Siegfried must die, and he is murdered.

Following is an account of how the sources differ in detail on these points.

1. *Siegfried woos Brunhild for Gunther.* The part of *Brot* which could have dealt with the matter is missing. In *Gripisspá* Griper predicts a swearing of love oaths between Sigurd and Brynhild, but no actual physical relationship occurs. Sigurd is to be 'ensnared' by Grimhild into forgetting Brynhild and wooing her on Gunnar's behalf, while he himself takes Gudrun as wife. *Skamma* says that '. . . they rode to propose to Brynhild', describing how Sigurd laid his sword between himself and the maiden and did not touch her, but mentioning neither magically-induced forgetfulness nor a disguise.

Of the epics the NL, which is alone among the sources in unequivocally dispensing with any prior acquaintance between Siegfried and Brunhild, offers the least complicated explanation of how Siegfried came to woo Brunhild for Gunther; Siegfried, having journeyed to Burgundy, falls in love with Kriemhild and offers to win Brunhild for Gunther if he in turn may wed Gunther's sister. Here the two proposed marriages constitute a mutual bargain: Siegfried may wed Kriemhild in exchange for acquiring Brunhild for Gunther, while in the North Sigurd's wooing of Brynhild on Gunnar's behalf is done, on the mother Grimhild's suggestion, after Sigurd has been married to Gudrun for some time.

In the VS Sigurd's marriage to Gudrun results from the machinations of the Giukungs' mother, Queen Grimhild, who according to *Gripisspá* would 'ensnare' Sigurd into forgetting Brynhild, with whom he has plighted his troth, so that he could wed Gudrun instead. In the saga she does this with a magic potion that erases all memory of Sigurd's previous relationship with Brynhild:

> [Sigurd] took the horn and drank from it. Grimhild said: 'King Giuki shall be your father and I your mother; Gunnar and Hogni shall swear oaths of brotherhood with you, and then there will not be found anyone to compare with the three of you.' Sigurd took these words well; but after the drink he no longer remembered Brynhild.

Disguised as Gunnar, Sigurd braves the wall of flame surrounding Brynhild's mountain home to woo her for Gunnar. This deceit is compounded by the fact that Brynhild is tricked not only into wedding the wrong man, but also into breaking her own oath to marry only the man who braves the flames. A similar trick figures in the NL, with two differences: the challenge to win Brunhild involves not heroism but strength – the prospective suitor must best Brunhild in a series of sporting events – and Siegfried competes not in disguise but made invisible by a magic cloak won from the Nibelungs, performing the actual feats while Gunther goes through the motions.

Compared to the other two epics the Ths. account lacks unity and consistency. Having arrived at Brynhild's castle, met her and tamed the horse Grane, Sigurd continues to Gunnar's kingdom and is married to Gunnar's sister Grimhild. Only in retrospect is a promise of Sigurd to marry Brynhild mentioned – by Brynhild herself when Sigurd returns to propose on behalf of Gunnar – and the promise plays no further role in the work. Here a disguise is dispensed with, Sigurd merely appearing in the role of negotiator on Gunnar's behalf, explaining to Brynhild, when she reminds him of his earlier promise to marry only her, that Grimhild was a better match for him because she had a brother.

2. *Brunhild learns something upsetting concerning the circumstances under which she was wooed and won for Gunther, during a prestige quarrel which arises between the two wives*. Rooted as it is in history, this quarrel must be quite an early feature in the Siegfried legend; yet the only evidence we have of its mention in the Eddic poetry is in the *Ride to Hel* in which Brynhild informs the Giantess that Gudrun had reproached her for having slept in Sigurd's arms, a tantalising reference to what must have formed a most important account of the quarrel in a now-lost source such as *Brot*.

In the Ths. we have already noted Sigurd's promise to Brynhild to marry no one else but her. After he has courted her on Gunnar's behalf and the pair have been married, Brynhild's superior strength prevents Gunnar from taking her virginity; accordingly Sigurd is empowered by Gunnar to do the deed, and made to swear an oath of secrecy about it. However, Sigurd later gives his wife the ring he took from Brynhild as a token of having deflowered her. When later a quarrel arises between the two women over who enjoys the more eminent position, Grimhild produces the ring and thereby reveals the truth to Brynhild. Thus in the one act of surrendering the ring to Grimhild, Sigurd is guilty of the double crime of breaking his oath of secrecy and, thereby, precipitating the gross insult to Brynhild's honour.[2]

In the NL the episode of Siegfried's boasting to his wife of having taken Brunhild's virginity to some extent parallels that in the Ths. Here, too, Gunther is unable to consummate his marriage with Brunhild. When Gunther confides the humiliating story of his disastrous wedding night to Siegfried the latter promises to subdue Brunhild so that Gunther can enjoy her, but not to make love to her himself. Made invisible by his magic cloak he enters the nuptial chamber and with his superior strength overcomes the girl so that she, believing it is Gunther, agrees to submit to her husband.

At this point the parallels with the straightforward Ths. version cease, for with his description of what transpired next the NL poet raises the perplexing question of whether or not Siegfried did then deflower Brunhild:

> Siegfried left the maiden lying there and stepped aside as though to remove his clothes and, without the noble Queen's noticing it, he drew a golden ring from her finger and then took her girdle . . . I do not know whether it was his pride which made him do it. Later he gave them to his wife . . .[3]

It is likely that the poet was being diplomatically unclear about what actually happened because he wanted to tone down the episode from the earlier versions in order to suit the tastes of his own audience: the Christian ladies and gentlemen of a mediaeval Austro-Bavarian court would not accept such improprieties as a chivalrous hero deflowering his brother-in-law's wife.[4] Thus the poet is neither admitting openly that the hero did so, nor explicitly denying that he did. The result is that the episode, taken as it stands, is tantalisingly ambiguous as to the extent of Siegfried's guilt.

One thing, nevertheless, is clear: if Siegfried did not deflower Brunhild, at the least he was at fault, as he was in the Ths., for surrendering to his wife the tokens of Brunhild's virginity. Thus while any jealousy motive is absent, Brunhild never having been in love with Siegfried, the question of honour still remains significant. 'If Siegfried has boasted of it, it will cost him his life,' thinks Brunhild after Kriemhild triumphantly reveals what she believes to be the truth.[5]

The VS, on the other hand, completely lacks the sexual episode and resultant offence to Brynhild's honour. Rather, it is the plain fact of the deceit perpetrated at her expense – that she has been tricked into marrying a different man from the great hero whom she swore to wed – which outrages Brynhild. Here it is the broken oaths which are emphasised: Sigurd's faithlessness to his own oaths to Brynhild, as well as his causing her to break her oath. In this connection it is important and interesting to note that, according to the ethical code of the Nordic people at the times these legends were current, oath-breaking was considered one of the most evil of crimes: in the Eddic poem *Völuspá* oath-breakers and murderers are singled out for punishment in the after-life. As one historian explains:

> Fidelity, or fealty, is a difficult, vague word. In general, it expressed the trust that men placed in each other: it made living together possible. That is why loyalty to one's oath was counted the greatest of virtues by all barbarians. [6]

3. *Brunhild decides that Siegfried must die, and he is murdered.* In *Gripisspá* Griper predicts that Brynhild, angered because Sigurd has not kept his promise to marry her, will incite Gunnar to murder Sigurd by lying that he had broken his brotherhood oath when sleeping with her during the three nights of wooing on the mountain. Neither *Brot* nor *Skamma*, on the other hand, tells us to what extent Sigurd's actions during a previous acquaintance between himself and Brynhild may have played a role in his murder – what, if anything, he has done to justify Brynhild's jealousy; the relevant part of *Brot* is missing, and as *Skamma* begins with Sigurd's arrival at Giuki's court any mention of a previous acquaintance between him and Brynhild is limited to vague allusions. In both poems the prime force behind|Sigurd's death is Brynhild's jealousy: she would rather have been wed to Sigurd than to Gunnar, and cannot bear to see Gudrun happily wed to him. But in *Brot* Brynhild eggs Gunnar on to the murder by falsely declaring (as in *Gripisspá*) that Sigurd has been untrue to his brotherhood oath (once Sigurd is dead she admits the lie), while in *Skamma* she incites Gunnar to the slaying by stirring up his desire to take over Sigurd's wealth and power.

In the VS Sigurd is slain because of his infidelity to his oath to

Brynhild and his role in causing her to break her own oath:
angered by these broken oaths Brynhild decides that Sigurd
shall be murdered. In the Ths., too, faithlessness to an oath
plays a role, but to this is added the insult to Brynhild's honour;
as Brynhild relates to Gunnar and Hogni the mortifying
incident of Grimhild's revelation the decision is immediately
taken to have revenge on Sigurd. The NL, as already seen, is
ambiguous about Siegfried's guilt in taking Brunhild's
virginity, but this is irrelevant: the fact remains that he handed
over to Kriemhild Brunhild's ring and girdle, 'leaving their
silent accusation uncorrected'.[7] It is from this act that his death
proceeds, the deed for which Brunhild vows that he will die;
compare Hagen's parallel statement, 'His boast that he
enjoyed my dear lady will cost him his life.'[8]

Thus the hero meets his end as retribution for real or alleged
offences. However, the fact that in *Skamma* Gunnar is incited
to the slaying through his coveting of Sigurd's wealth and
power returns us to the important point previously made,
namely that while this retribution is the overt reason for his
death, the real motive for doing away with him is a desire for his
treasure and power.

In the literature – unlike in *The Ring* where all of the treasure
in Siegfried's possession became his through his victory over
Fafner – the hero's treasure originates from more than one
source. To be sure, the most important part of it was won from
the dragon, but some was acquired in more 'conventional'
ways: inherited from his father (in the Ths.), as booty in war
campaigns embarked upon with Gunther/Gunnar and his
family, or as part of a dowry for marrying their sister.

The Ths. reviews many of Sigurd's war campaigns in detail,
while the VS recounts that he, with the Giukungs,

> now travelled widely throughout the lands and did many a brave
> deed; they slew many kings' sons, and no other men
> accomplished such wonderful things as they did . . .

An important treasure source is the dowry, for this implies

not merely wealth for its own sake but power, specifically, political power, and even more to the point, *shared political power* which, as we have seen in the case of the Merovingians, all too easily lends itself to internal strife: in Sigurd's case, co-rulership of Gunnar's dominion. *Skamma* relates:

> A maiden [Gudrun] they gave him
> and wealth untold . . .

In the VS Gunnar promises Sigurd, 'There is much we would give you so that you remain here long, both power and sovereignty and, of our own will, our sister . . . ' while in the Ths. Sigurd receives half of Gunnar's kingdom as dowry upon his marriage to Grimhild.

The NL both preserves the concept of the treasure as booty taken in war – Siegfried seizes it after doing battle with and slaying many of the Nibelungs (who here are ordinary men, not elves) – and maintains the association of the treasure with political power: the possessor of the treasure is Lord of Nibelungland.

That wealth came to symbolise power is readily understandable: the notion of acquiring vast riches is an attractive one, and when history became saga an abstract or complex concept such as political advancement could be translated into the simpler, and ever more fascinating, idea of acquisition of a treasure. Instances of this can even be found in books designed to relate history rather than legend, for example in Gregory of Tours' account of Aëtius' actions following the battle on the Catalaunian Plains:

> When the battle was over, Aëtius said to Thorismund [son of the King of the Goths]: 'Now you must go back home quickly, for otherwise you will be cheated out of your father's kingdom by the machinations of your brother.' Thorismund hurried off as soon as he received this advice, hoping to forestall his brother and to occupy their father's throne before him. By a similar stratagem Aëtius persuaded the King of the Franks to leave. [9]

The reason for Aëtius' having persuaded the various barbarian chieftains to return home was because they were eager to pursue the Huns in a fight to the finish which, as we have seen, Aëtius wanted to avoid: 'Never, out of pride and without compelling reasons, destroy an opponent for whom you might once again have use.'[10] Gregory,[11] however, continues the tale thus:

> As soon as they [Thorismund and the Frankish king], had both gone, Aëtius collected all the booty lying about on the field of battle and set off with it for home.

Whatever the inspiration behind Gregory's version, it illustrates the readiness with which people have adopted the treasure motive as a means of explaining and understanding the actions of others.

The identification of the treasure with power deepens its significance as a motive for Siegfried's murder, and thus it is that the treasure-acquisition motive, which generally symbolises a bid for increased political strength, must be balanced against the vengeance motive with respect to the relative importance of each as a reason for wanting Siegfried eliminated.

One of the most clear-cut sources on both points is *Skamma*. In urging Gunnar to slay Sigurd Brynhild appeals exclusively to Gunnar's desire for power: the idea of a (real or alleged) crime of Sigurd's that demands vengeance never enters the picture, at least not from the point of view of Gunnar, who arranges the murder; whatever reasons Brynhild may have, pertaining to Sigurd's actions, for wanting him eliminated we are not specifically told, only given to know that she is jealous of Gudrun. In the conversation with Gunnar she plunges immediately into threats:

> You, O Gunnar, stand to lose
> the lands I own and me myself;
> life holds no joy for me, living with you.

> I will return to the land of my father,
> back to my friends, back to my kinsmen;
> there I shall sit and spend my time sleeping,
> if you slay not Sigurd the mighty,
> taking his place as greatest of princes.

Gunnar, saddened by the prospect of having to harm his blood-brother, is nonetheless even more concerned over the possible detriment to his own reputation if he does not act as Brynhild demands:

> Gunnar weighed the matter with care;
> it was not a normal thing
> for a queen to forsake throne and husband.

The prospect of losing not only Brynhild but also her dowry (*i.e.* the part of her father's kingdom which is her birthright) confirms his resolve:

> Gladly will I lay down my life
> rather than forfeit that maiden's treasures.

He then puts the matter to Hogni; like Brynhild Gunnar minces no words:

> Shall we slay Sigurd to better our lot?
> Good it is to control the Rhine's metal
> and peacefully to enjoy
> the security brought by such wealth.

Thus the reasons for Sigurd's murder in *Skamma* are purely political: Gunnar wants to salvage his own reputation and indeed to enhance it by doing away with someone who, while officially a co-ruler (Sigurd having been granted a share in the rule of Gunnar's kingdom upon his marriage to Gudrun), is, because of his pre-eminence in wealth and heroism, in effect a rival. This rivalry is implied in the last two lines quoted above, *i.e.* that Gunnar will feel happier and more peaceful if the sovereignty of the land is kept within the family. It is not merely a matter of a greedy desire to steal what is essentially Sigurd's wealth, but rather a political ambition to eliminate Sigurd as co-ruler and thereby appropriate *all* the power (and consequently all the jointly-owned wealth) for himself.

In the VS Brynhild repeats the threat she has made in *Skamma*. Again Gunnar grows 'sick at heart' at the suggestion of killing someone to whom he is bound by oath, but finally he thinks of how shameful it will be if his wife left him. Of his own accord, and not through a suggestion of Brynhild, he reaches the conclusion that he could increase his power and wealth with Sigurd dead, and mentions it immediately to Hogni:

> 'Trouble is heavy on me,' and [Gunnar] tells [Hogni] that he must needs slay Sigurd, for that he has failed him wherein he trusted him; 'so let us be lords of the gold and the realm withal.'[12]

Seen in this context Gunnar's desire for increased power and wealth (as well as the concern for his reputation) becomes the real reason for wanting Sigurd out of the way and the vengeance for Sigurd's 'betrayal' of Gunnar and Brynhild a pretext.

The NL is more complex than the other sources on this issue. It is difficult to know what is uppermost in the mind of Hagen, who is the most determined to have Siegfried out of the way and himself commits the murder: the avenging of Brynhild's outraged honour or the acquisition of more power for the Burgundians. They seem to weigh equally – the one not being merely an excuse for the other – and in a sense the former could be said to be subsumed under the latter, for a truly great King should not suffer his Queen to be insulted in this way. What is obvious, though, is that Hagen's interest in the treasure, both before and after Siegfried's death, is motivated not by greed but by the political might it confers: firstly, there is a magic wand which confers unlimited power, and secondly, the fact that the lord of the treasure is lord of Nibelungland; and thirdly, his reason for wanting to remove the treasure from the widow's possession is that she is using it to recruit warriors who might be used against the Burgundians. Nonetheless, Hagen could not act on his own account without Gunther's consent in the matter, and thus it is Gunther's attitude that is decisive.

Gunther is not interested in avenging Siegfried's 'crime' because he alone knows the true circumstances and is thus satisfied that Siegfried is not guilty. It is only when Hagen presents the possibility of increased Burgundian royal power that Gunther finally lets himself be persuaded to consent to the plot against Siegfried. When Hagen first comes with this suggestion Gunther grows 'very despondent',[13] but later, after asking for and receiving detailed assurances from Hagen as to how the plan could succeed, 'the King followed his vassal Hagen's advice, . . . and those rare knights began to set afoot the great betrayal before any might discover it'.[14]

Wagner weaves his way through the complexities of the different versions of the affair as presented in the sources to fashion, from the sticky threads of personal retribution and political ambition, his own web of intrigue in which the hero shall be ensnared. Sovereignty held in common, deceit connected with arranged marriages, power lust – all of these themes form a continuous link from history through legend to the text of *The Ring*.

Just as the sharing of sovereignty was the root of most (if not all) evil in the stormy centuries when the Merovingian brother-kings ruled the Frankish realm, so too did the legendary Siegfried's entry into Gunther's court and swearing of brotherhood oaths with him spell his perdition. Nor has Wagner's hero escaped the political pitfall of shared sovereignty, an arrangement reflected in Gunther's welcoming words to Siegfried, and the hero's reply to him, in *Götterdämmerung* Act I:

> Gunther: O hero, greet with joy the home of my father.
> Wherever you walk, whatever you see,
> regard as your own:
> yours is my inheritance, my land and my people:
> my body, support my oath!
> I offer myself as your man.
>
> Siegfried: Neither land nor people can I offer,
> nor father's house or estate:
> all I inherited was my own body;
> while I live I use it up.
> I have only a sword which I forged myself:
> my sword, support my oath!
> With myself I offer it to our alliance.

That the Gibichungs share in the power conferred by Siegfried's treasure is represented by the fact that not Siegfried but Hagen knows how to make use of it. The knowledge of the power of the ring Hagen keeps a secret, but, because it will eventually serve his own ends, he does tell Siegfried about the properties of the Tarnhelm:[15]

> The Tarnhelm I know, the Niblungs' cleverest work:
> if you put it on your head, it changes you
> into any shape;
> if you want to be in the farthest place,
> it takes you there instantly.

Once the Gibichungs have secured Siegfried's friendship the stage is set for the *marriage bargain*, which in *The Ring*, as in the NL, is a mutual one: Siegfried may wed Gutrune in return for winning Brünnhilde for Gunther. First, from the VS comes the magic drink of forgetfulness, a simple and obvious dramatic device of transition from the Brünnhilde to the Gutrune relationship. In the saga, however, the return of Sigurd's memory – an event which occurs at a much earlier stage than in *The Ring* – is a completely internalised event with no visible consequences and needing no help from a new potion:

> When [Gunnar and Brynhild's wedding feast] was at an end,
> Sigurd remembered all the oaths he had sworn to Brynhild;
> nevertheless he let things remain as they were.

This was hardly of dramatic value for Wagner. Instead the return of Siegfried's memory becomes the occasion on which his previous relationship with Brünnhilde is suddenly revealed to a shocked Gunther and his vassals; moreover, a dramatic symmetry is imparted to the plot in that the recovery of Siegfried's memory is induced by a drink from Hagen just as the loss of it was.

In the NL and Ths. the discovery of the deed of which the hero is accused – whether it be infidelity to a brotherhood oath or an insult to Brunhild's honour – is ultimately brought about by his carelessness in taking Brunhild's ring (and in the NL her girdle as well) and handing it over as a trophy to his wife. Wagner adapted this slip-up of Siegfried's for much the same purpose. For the sake of compression of the plot Siegfried does not give the ring to Gutrune for her to exhibit at a later time, but keeps it himself instead of surrendering it to Gunther as,

for the sake of consistency, he should have done; here
Brünnhilde's discovery, immediately upon her arrival in
Gunther's land, of the ring on Siegfried's finger, when it should
have been on Gunther's, precipitates her accusation of
Siegfried's infidelity in the sense that she then realises that it
was Siegfried and not Gunther who came to her mountain the
second time.

That Siegfried stands formally accused of an act he did not
commit – disloyalty to Gunther in making love to Gunther's
intended bride – results from the confusion unwittingly caused
by people talking at cross purposes. Upon her arrival at the
Gibichung court Brünnhilde, seeing Siegfried, declares that he
has betrayed her: he himself had married her with the ring as a
token, and made love to her:

> Then all of you, know this:
> not this man [Gunther]
> but that man there [Siegfried]
> is my husband . . .
> He forced pleasure and love from me.

All the witnesses (except Hagen, who knows the truth),
unaware of any previous acquaintance between Siegfried and
Brünnhilde, assume that this was supposed to have occurred
during the time when he was courting her on Gunther's behalf,
while actually she is referring to events farther back in time,
before he left her fire-protected mountain in search of new
adventures. This confusion reaches its climax in the double-
meanings attached to certain key words in the heated exchange
between the two protagonists:

> Siegfried:      Nothung, the worthy sword,
> guarded the oath of loyalty;
> its sharp edge separated me
> from this poor woman.
>
> Brünnhilde:   You cunning hero, see how you lie!
> How well I know its sharpness,
> but I also know the sheath
> in which Nothung, the faithful friend,
> so blissfully rested on the wall
> when its master courted his beloved.

The German word for sheath, 'Scheide', can also mean the female sex organ; in such a context, 'Schwert' (= 'sword') assumes the significance of a phallic symbol.

This confusion was taken by Wagner from the VS. Brynhild, in egging Gunnar on to the murder of Sigurd, declares, 'Sigurd has betrayed me, and you as well, since you let him come into my bed.' Does she mean that Sigurd deceitfully won Gunnar a bride who had already been promised to someone else (*i.e.* himself), or is she deliberately misleading Gunnar as she does in the *Edda*, making him believe that Sigurd made love to her during the time he spent winning her as a bride for him?[16] What is important for Sigurd's subsequent fate – as well as for Wagner's purposes – is that *Gunnar construes Brynhild's words as meaning that she and Sigurd had made love during the time he was wooing her for Gunnar*, for later Gunnar reflects on how Sigurd 'failed him wherein he trusted him,' and for this reason he consents to the murder. Thus Wagner's Gunther similarly misconstrues Brünnhilde's declaration, 'He forced pleasure and love from me,' and the confusion results which is resolved only by Siegfried's death.

In the epic poems the revelation of the hero's (real or alleged) crime is occasioned by the confrontation between the two wives, which especially in the NL is quite dramatic. Wagner, playing down the female quarrel because his two women are not equal in stature, omits this episode,[17] but retains the spirit and the drama of it by permitting instead an open confrontation between Siegfried and Brünnhilde in the swearing of oaths on Hagen's spear. This scene as such does not appear in any of the sources, but Wagner derived the idea from the NL, the only source in which Siegfried is given a chance to defend himself; there Siegfried, after Brunhild's accusation, offers to swear an oath in the presence of Gunther's vassals as to his innocence:

> [King Gunther said,] 'You must give us proof of that. If the oath you offer is duly sworn here I shall clear you of all treason.' And he commanded the proud Burgundians to stand in a ring. Brave

Siegfried raised his hand to swear but the mighty king said: 'Your great innocence is so well known to me that I acquit you of my sister's allegation and accept that you are not guilty of the deed.'[18]

Thus has the web of intrigue inexorably tightened around Siegfried, and his end is plotted, ostensibly to avenge his infidelity to his oaths – to Brünnhilde on the one hand and Gunther on the other – and yet once again does ambition for power and wealth stalk across the picture, in the same way as in the NL, when the reluctant Gunther is won over to the conspiracy as Hagen points out the gain to be enjoyed with Siegfried eliminated:

> Hagen: Our only help is –Siegfried's death!
>
> Gunther (shuddering): Siegfried's death!
>
> Hagen: Only that can avenge your shame!
>
> Gunther: We swore blood-brotherhood together.
>
> Hagen: Only blood can avenge the breaking of the oath.
>
> Gunther: Did he break the oath?
>
> Hagen: He did when he betrayed you.
>
> . . . .
>
> He shall fall – to your advantage!
> Unheard-of power will be yours
> if you win from him the ring,
> which can be done only through his death.
>
> Gunther: Brünnhilde's ring?
>
> Hagen: The Nibelung's ring!
>
> Gunther: So let it be, the end of Siegfried!

Therefore the 'technical' reason for murdering Siegfried is to avenge the breaking of his oath. Depending on one's point of view, the reason is twofold: from Brünnhilde's viewpoint, Siegfried's infidelity to her; from the Gibichungs', his breaking of the blood-brotherhood oath he swore to Gunther. If Siegfried's alleged infidelity – to Gunther on one hand and Brünnhilde on the other – is the 'technical' reason for his downfall, then the true, overriding motive for it is greed for his treasure and for the power conferred by the ring.

So much for other people's reasons for wanting Siegfried out of the way. But now it is time to pick up the discussion anticipated at the end of Chapter Two, and discover to what extent, if any, Siegfried himself bears the responsibility for his own downfall. Is he simply brought down as an innocent victim of an evil conspiracy, 'framed' on trumped-up charges, or does he bear his own measure of guilt?

Here we can disregard the effects of Hagen's magic drink, or the confusion that resulted from Brünnhilde's accusation, 'He forced pleasure and love from me,' which caused Gunther to draw the wrong conclusions. The real crux of the matter is the deceit involved in Siegfried's wooing of Brünnhilde while disguised as Gunther. Here we have not Brunechild's husband Sigebert, assassinated in the course of a feud in which he essentially took no part, but Chilperich, negotiating for the hand of Galswintha under the false pretences of bestowing on her all the respect and prestige due to the King's consort. Therefore the essential, mythical heroism of the bride-winning motif has, in its second appearance both in the sources and in *The Ring*, been tarnished by historically-rooted concepts of politically convenient marriages, of compulsion, of deceit.[19]

Moreover, this dishonesty occurs in conjunction with the exercise of power. Having won the treasure from Fafner Siegfried is now Lord of the Nibelungs, an idea which Wagner retained from the NL. In the 1848 prose sketch Siegfried actually refers to himself by that title, but it does not appear in the final version; with its historically-rooted implications of a temporal-political sovereignty it was superfluous for Wagner's purposes. What is important is that Siegfried uses his power for a fraudulent purpose: to quote the sketch of 1848, he 'exercises for the first and only time his power as Lord of the Nibelungs, by putting on the Tarnhelm and using it to disguise himself as Gunther'.[20] He thus goes against everything for which he was destined. Indeed, he not only deludes Brünnhilde into marrying the wrong man but also (which comes particularly from the NL) helps Gunther to enhance his reputation on the false grounds of having won Brünnhilde himself. Further, his actions precipitate a situation characterised by *absence of love* as well as *compulsion*, for Brünnhilde is being forced into something against her will.

And in what context did Siegfried perform these actions? Under the terms of a blood-brotherhood oath with Gunther. He has thus repeated Wotan's mistake and *entered into a treaty*: he is no longer a free man. As Dr. Wapnewski comments, 'Irony could not work more cruelly,'[21] when Siegfried, in Gunther's guise, presents himself to Brünnhilde with the words, 'Ein Freier kam!' 'Freier' in this context means a 'wooer' or 'suitor', but the word could also mean 'a free man' – just now, anything but an apt description. At this point it becomes manifest how Wagner has transformed the original mythical-religious significance of the Valkyrie's runes into a vehicle for conveying his own message. Knowledge – truth – makes one free. Siegfried, as a fearless hero, has had access to the highest teachings, yet he has disregarded them, involved himself with the Gibichungs and thereby become unfree.

Thus Wagner has unravelled the complicated webs of historico-legendary intrigues to formulate a drama with a significant message: to show how Siegfried uses – or abuses – power.

Siegfried has exercised power for the sole time for a corrupt purpose, and moreover, he has done this in the context of denying his own freedom through entering a treaty. The ultimate outcome is his downfall. Thus Wagner's intended *mythical* hero has, through his one fatal flaw inspired by historically-rooted intrigues, metamorphosed into a *tragic* hero in true Greek style:[22] he falls, not only victim to the intrigues of others, but through his own fault. The nineteenth-century philologist Wilhelm Müller[23] gave the following allegorical interpretation of the Siegfried legend, which cannot have failed to influence Wagner:

As long as he [Sigurd] follows the young warrior maiden (Brynhild) whom he has awakened from sleep, he is victorious through strength and wisdom. Malice (Grimhild) leads him into the arms of lust (Gudrun) and lures him into forgetting the call of the Valkyrie. Now his luck forsakes him. The sons of darkness (the Nibelungs) overpower him.

Siegfried's downfall, then, states Müller, springs from poetic justice. It can even be maintained that Siegfried's involvement with corruption, and his resultant death, spring not so much either from myth or from recorded history as from human nature itself.

## Notes

1. Wallace-Hadrill, *The Long-haired Kings*, p. 230.

2. The question naturally arises of whether the memory of Sigurd's broken promises of marriage could also have been part of the reason for Brynhild's desire for revenge on Sigurd.

3. p. 93.

4. Hatto, NL, p. 299.

5. NL, p. 114.

6. Wallace-Hadrill, *The Barbarian West*, p. 104.

7. p. 329.

8. p. 117.

9. p. 118.

10. Riehl, p.196.

11. p. 118.

12. VS, p. 187.

13. NL, p. 117.

14. NL, p. 118.

15. In the NL, too, Hagen knows of the magic wand which confers unlimited power on its owner, while Siegfried either does not seem to be aware of it, or if he is, does not care about it.

16. One of the inconsistencies of the saga is that in her accusation of faithlessness Brynhild does not take into account the effects of the magic potion, although she knows about the drink. Perhaps she is specifically angry about Sigurd's failure to correct the situation once his memory has returned?

17. A fragment of it does survive in *The Ring*, see Chapter Three.

18. p. 116. Gunther's expressed willingness to take Siegfried's innocence for granted must be understood in terms of his anxiety that the secret of Siegfried's subduing of Brunhild be kept.

19. Indeed, in the NL heroism has degenerated into a mere display of physical prowess.

20. 'Der Nibelungenmythus.'

21. p. 142.

22. The Greek tragedies, of which many were to be found in Wagner's library, were very influential in the shaping of his work.

23. pp. 10f.

5

# Son of Darkness

Hagen is one of the most enigmatic figures of *The Ring*, a fascinating illustration of Dr. Wapnewski's observation on Wagner's heroes and villains:

> . . . and even the miserable and corrupt, the poor and the evil receive a bit of sympathy, yes, even respect, from the heart of this 'Orpheus of all secret misery' [as Nietzsche called Wagner]: thus to Alberich, Beckmesser, Loge, Melot – and even to Hagen's infamy and malice is a measure of greatness imparted; it is clear from the music . . . Wagner's villains are less villainous, and his heroes less heroic, than the tradition of interpreting these roles would have it. [1]

Thus if an occasional tendency towards oversimplification on the part of commentators as well as of artistic interpreters has made Hagen seem merely to be the villain of *The Ring*, an investigation of the sources from which he is derived will reveal him to be a far richer, more complex figure than this.

Hagen occupies a variety of roles in *Götterdämmerung*. First of all, he is set apart, different, with a tinge of inferiority – the half-brother, son of an elf. Secondly, he is possessed of extraordinary knowledge and wisdom (a product of his elfish ancestry), because of which he enjoys the position of his half-brother King Gunther's trusted adviser and confidant; but more than this, he is the power behind the throne, making and implementing the decisions for his weak king. Finally, Hagen is a betrayer, working against Gunther while appearing to act in his interests and, most importantly, slaying Siegfried, whom he envies, in order to gain the ring and the power it confers.

These roles and qualities have their roots in legend and ultimately in history. Tracing them can be a complex matter, for Hagen is one of those characters whose synthesis from two different traditions has to be accounted for: in the Siegfried tradition the murderer, or instigator of the murder, of the hero; and in the saga of the Burgundian downfall the trusted adviser and assistant to the royal family.

The fusion of the two traditions into one legend necessarily brought about the identification of certain characters in the one tradition with certain, logical counterparts in the other. One can presume that the original characters in each tradition must have had some similar qualities for the identification to have been made. Possibly it happened like this:

1.  The legend of the Burgundian downfall contained a character who was a trusted adviser to the Burgundian King Gundahari or Gunther. In this capacity he got the Burgundians into the situation that resulted in their destruction; possibly he was secretly allied with the agent of their downfall.

2.  The Siegfried legend featured someone responsible for the treacherous murder of Siegfried, who either actually carried out the murder or who was powerful enough to instigate it.

3.  When the two legends were combined it would have been natural for the betrayer of Siegfried to become identified with the adviser to the Burgundians who, in effect, betrayed his masters. Similar motives for the two deeds may have strengthened the identification, for example that Siegfried was murdered for his treasure and that the Burgundians too were destroyed because their adversary desired their treasure.

Wagner intended Hagen to be Siegfried's 'dark' counterpart. To achieve the right balance between the two figures it was necessary for Wagner to accentuate those negative qualities of Hagen that are hinted at in the sources. Nevertheless we should not lose sight of the fact – as Wagner indeed did not – that Hagen's forbears, in history as well as in the literary sources, were men of outstanding heroism in their own right.

An obvious outlet for heroism exists in situations of a military nature, and in fact the 'military' aspect of the Hagen figure would seem to have been a consistent feature, particularly in the German branch of the legend, and survives in Hagen's officiating at the head of the Burgundian army in the NL and Ths. and ultimately in the *Ring* scene in which Hagen summons the Vassals. Thus it is not surprising that for two of the earliest models for the 'Burgundian' Hagen we must turn to the latter part of the fourth century and the first half of the fifth for two commanders in the Roman army whose lives were strikingly similar with respect to features that eventually formed a part of the Hagen figure. One of these was the illustrious general *Flavius Stilicho (ca. 365-408)*, the other his protegé *Flavius Aëtius (ca. 390-454)*. These two men, through both their military prowess and their expertise as statesmen, made themselves indispensable to the weak Roman emperors they served, just as Hagen in the NL and *The Ring* is indispensable to the weak and indecisive Gunther. For example, Stilicho decisively repelled the Visigoths under their king Alarich in 403, a feat which earned him the reputation of saviour of the fatherland. In 451 Aëtius effectively put an end to the power of the Huns in the West by leading an army composed of the united barbarian nations against Attila's Huns in the battle on the Catalaunian Plains.

It was Aëtius who figured in the event which had direct bearing on the Burgundian saga, for in 435 (to quote from the chronicle of Prosper of Aquitaine) 'Aëtius crushed in battle Gunther, the king of the Burgundians, who lived in the interior of the Gauls, and granted him peace at his prayer'. A year or two later the Huns came and totally annihilated the Burgundians, king and all. It is not known for certain whether

**Germanic warrior from the Heroic Age.**

this was done with the tacit consent of Aëtius, but it is likely anyway that the two battles became mingled in popular memory, the more so because the army of Aëtius consisted largely of Hunnish troops (having been a hostage of the Huns in his youth – see footnote 3 – he knew how to use this experience to his best advantage).

Important to the development of the Hagen figure is that the very achievements which made them indispensable to their emperors caused them to be suspected of *double-dealing*, indeed virtually of treason. In his encounter with Alarich Stilicho did not crush the Visigoths entirely as he could have done: his policy was never to destroy, without compelling reasons, an opponent who might later once more prove useful. Consequently he was suspected of plotting to take over the power of Rome for himself, setting up himself or his son as Emperor, possibly with the assistance of the allied barbarian tribes.

Similarly Aëtius, taking a leaf from his mentor's book, did not annihilate the Huns completely on the Catalaunian Plains but allowed them to retreat. Indeed, the sense of not knowing where one had Aëtius was one of his most important characteristics to be incorporated into the Hagen figure. Aëtius was viewed this way both by the powers in Rome whose military commander he was and by the barbarian tribes with whom he dealt. In the great battle against the Huns Aëtius was seen not only as turning against his former allies (indeed at one stage of his career Aëtius had his own private army of Hunnish soldiers), but, because he let the Huns retreat, he was regarded by Rome with considerable suspicion and reproached for giving his contacts with the Huns priority over the interests of the Empire for the sake of personal gain. In actual fact, however, Aëtius was thinking not only in military but also in political terms: he knew that from a total defeat of the Huns would arise the danger that the barbarian nations, now united, might turn against Rome, whereas a continued threat from the Huns would serve to ensure the alliance between Rome and the

German tribes. Here, then, we can anticipate not only Hagen, the *skilful politician* of the NL, indispensable aid to his king, but also the *betrayer*, the man responsible for the Burgundian downfall. That these seemingly conflicting traits could be incorporated into one and the same character would stem from the different attitudes of the peoples among whom the legends formed to the historical models: whether, for example, they were inclined to regard Aëtius as a traitor or a hero.

As a result of later historical events Attila took over the role of agent of the Burgundian defeat; consequently, the role of the Hagen figure in the holocaust grew more complex. While the character was now more firmly established in the 'Burgundian camp', as it were, he still retained a trace of his inimical relationship to them: here we can recall that view (see Chapter One) which attributes to the NL Hagen the essential responsibility for the fall of the Burgundians (reflected in *The Ring* through Hagen's slaying of Gunther), for had he voluntarily surrendered himself to Kriemhild's avenging sword the holocaust would never have taken place. Thus it is possible that this apparent responsibility of Hagen's is a survival of a very early, pre-Attila tradition which regarded the Burgundian downfall as something of an 'inside job', a tendency to regard the person responsible as a traitor.[2]

Another attribute of Stilicho and Aëtius to have survived in an aspect of the Hagen figure is that both men were partly *foreigners*: Stilicho was Roman on his mother's side and Vandal on his father's, while Aëtius' mother was a wealthy, noble Roman and his father a barbarian – a quality which survives in the NL Hagen's and Ths. Hogni's designation by the name of their birthplace – 'of Tronje' or 'Troja' – to indicate their origin outside the place of action, and in the half-brother, half-elf status of the Ths. Hogni and Wagner's Hagen, both of whom sustain an insult from their royal half-brother referring to their unusual origin.[3]

While the colourful careers of these two Roman army commanders gave the initial impulse for the development of the Hagen figure in the Burgundian legend, that development was later furthered by the Franks who took over the lands formerly occupied by the defeated Burgundians. In the sixth-century Frankish kingdom there lived a man whose own life made no small contribution to the character of Hagen. This was *Eunius Mummolus*. Raised to the rank of patrician by King Guntram, Mummolus advanced steadily in the service of the King and was appointed to increasingly important posts. Above all he distinguished himself as a *military leader*, mobilising a Gaulish army against Langobard attackers and later subduing the Saxons and making them swear a fealty oath to the Frankish King. He was always victorious in his campaigns.

Later Mummolus *deserted Guntram* and espoused the cause of Gundovald the Pretender. During the siege of Comminges in which Gundovald was opposed by Guntram's forces, Mummolus abandoned Gundovald in exchange for assurances from Guntram's side that his life would be spared. Despite these assurances, however, the order was given that Mummolus and his chief allies should be put to death. As Gregory of Tours[4] describes the circumstances of Mummolus' last stand one cannot help but recall the scene of Hagen's death in the NL and Ths. Leudegisel, Guntram's Count of the Stables, had Mummolus in his hut.

> He emerged and immediately ordered the hut to be surrounded, so that Mummolus might be killed. For a long time Mummolus resisted his assailants, but in the end he came to the door. As he stepped out they ran him through from both sides with their lances. He fell dead to the ground.

Moreover, one wonders whether Guntram's order that Mummolus be put to death is not reflected in Gunnar's order in *Atlakvida* for Hogni's heart to be cut out.

Further, Mummolus and his wife had amassed a huge amount of *wealth*. His widow revealed to the King that there was 'a vast hoard of gold and silver . . . hidden in Avignon' which Mummolus 'had stolen . . . from some hoard of treasure which he had discovered'.[5]

A valuable assistant and military leader, later a deserter, resisting death at the hands of former allies, the keeper of a hidden hoard of treasure – Mummolus possessed the undeniable hallmarks of a Hagen figure. His life must have been a source of inspiration for those Merovingian court singers who re-fashioned the Burgundian saga for their own audiences.

Hagen's role as *power behind the throne*, which figures so importantly in the NL and *The Ring*, would not have been a significant part of the earliest forms of the Burgundian legend as the original King Gundahari was considered a mighty king in his own right and not a weakling. While the basis for this aspect of Hagen was laid in Stilicho's and Aëtius' relationships with the weak Roman emperors they served, it essentially owes its development and establishment to the later Merovingian period and the Merovingian office of Mayor of the Palace.

The office of Mayor of the Palace, or Palace Steward, first mentioned by Gregory of Tours in 581,[6] was filled by leading members of the aristocracy, the great land-owners. The Mayor ruled over the royal household and the army. His was a highly influential position, so much so that during the seventh and eighth centuries the Mayors gradually usurped the authority of the kings until the later Merovingian kings were completely under the thumb of their Mayors and, ultimately, the last of the Merovingians, Childeric III, was deposed by his Mayor of the Palace, Pepin the Short, in 754. It was natural that, as later Frankish singers and poets incorporated characteristics of their own weak kings into the originally heroic Burgundian Gundahari (see Chapter Six), the figure of Hagen would correspondingly assume the authority of a Mayor of the Palace, taking his place in the forefront of the administration of the kingdom.

Since the Hagen figure could claim such historical forbears as Stilicho and Aëtius who wielded the true reins of Roman power while their weak emperors occupied their ineffectual thrones, and the Merovingian Mayors of the Palace who fulfilled a similar but even more intensified relationship with their effete monarchs, it was inevitable that the Hagen-Gunther relationship should be influenced by the peoples' experience of various forms of *double kingship*. One important example of this form of government existed in the Khazar Empire, which flourished between the seventh and tenth centuries. The true king had no social intercourse with his people, but instead had a deputy who

> commands and supplies the armies, manages the affairs of state, appears in public and leads in war . . . [He has] the power to bind or release, to mete out punishment, and to govern the country . . .[7]

The king's title was Great Khagan, that of his deputy Khagan Bek, a name whose similarity to our Hagen is probably not mere coincidence, as we shall see. Yet again, with the roles of trusted assistant and of traitor seemingly inextricably linked in the Hagen figure of the Burgundian tradition, especially in the early versions, of even more immediate relevance to the evolution of the legend is the ancient Germanic tradition of hostile brothers:

> . . . A number of Germanic peoples had a pair of rulers, described as brothers, included among the ancestors of their royal house. The Vandals had two early kings called Raos and Raptos, the Langobards two heroes Ibor and Aio, and there are brother kings mentioned in the early history of the Swedes . . . The Anglo-Saxons had Hengest and Horsa . . . The idea that one brother kills the other, as in the case of the Roman twins, Romulus and Remus, is found as part of some of these traditions.[8]

These figures, though semi-mythical, were based on the historical practice of double kingship among some barbarian nations. The Huns, for example, had two periods of double kingship, in both of which one brother emerged as the dominant figure; best known were the brothers Attila and Bleda who 'at least nominally, reigned united and equally more than a decade'.[9] Attila deposed his brother in 445.

Still, a true full-brother relationship between Hagen and Gunther developed only in the Northern tradition. On the

Continent Hagen eventually emerged as a vassal of the king, probably through the original inspiration of the Merovingian concept of *leudes*. This is a Frankish word (the same as modern German 'Leute' = 'people') referring to 'the nobles who had sworn a special oath of loyalty to the king and from whom his personal bodyguard was formed'.[10] In 534 the *leudes* of one king, Theudebert, helped their master establish himself on his father's throne after the latter's death, thus foiling the attempts of his uncles to seize his kingdom. Entirely acceptable it was, furthermore, that such a person, as a member of the leading aristocracy (which also pertained to the later Mayors of the Palace), could be a distant kinsman of the king, as Hagen in the NL is.

Thus have we traced the principal streams of influence that contributed to the Hagen character of the Burgundian legend. In the Siegfried legend, particularly in the early stages of its formation, the concept of a *single individual opponent* of the hero may not have been important, all attention having been focused on the hero himself, his brave exploits and treacherous death. Thus it is entirely possible that the ancient forms of the Siegfried legend did not feature a single, prominent character in the role of 'Siegfried's' murderer. Indeed, the absence of a prominent Sigurd-murderer in the Nordic tradition may support the theory of the early hero's downfall through a group of conspirators: it is possible that the Siegfried legend reached the North before one outstanding individual assumed the role of his slayer.

If this assumption is true, then, in tracing the evolution of Hagen in his capacity as Siegfried's murderer we are not faced with the usual task of attempting to reconstruct the process by which a single legendary figure assumed a lasting form through the gradual acquisition of suitable attributes from appropriate historical persons. Instead we must seek why and when a group of possibly comparatively anonymous persons in a legend merged into, or were replaced by, a single, identifiable individual.

The Merovingian period is likely to yield part of the answer. The name of the assassin of King Sigebert has survived, and his name was – Chagan. Since this was the time when other principals of the Siegfried legend acquired their permanent names – Brunhild definitely, and possibly Siegfried if he did not already possess some form of that name – it is not unthinkable that Chagan too made a contribution in this respect, the existence and survival of a particular name leading to the identification of the hero's murderer(s) as a single individual. Furthermore, Chagan was a *foreigner*, of the fierce Asiatic tribe of the Avars, relatives of the Huns and undoubtedly a people for whom his name would have borne the connotation of *double kingship*. Therefore his entry into the Siegfried legend around the time of the merging with the Burgundian legend would also have made him a likely catalysing agent for the identification of that single murderer with the 'Hagen' figure of the Burgundian legend who shared similar qualities, while their roles as *traitors* in their respective legends and the *treasure motive* as a reason for their actions were other characteristics common to the Siegfried-murderer and the Burgundian adviser/assistant which led to the fusion of these two figures when the legends merged. But there was one overriding factor which bridged the gap between the two legends, providing a lasting mould in which the Hagen figure would be cast: it was the myth of Balder and Loki – the slaying of the beautiful god by the cunning and envious devil – which gave the legend of Siegfried and Hagen its final definition. This will be discussed in detail further on.

The sources universally regard Hagen as a hero – something which would not be obvious to anyone knowing him only from *The Ring*. Following in the footsteps of such historical forebears as Stilicho and Aëtius he appears consistently as an *eminent warrior* – in the NL he is called 'the boldest warrior that ever bore sword' and 'the best knight who ever bore shield to battle'[11] – and often appears in the NL and Ths. at the command of a vast army. As a warrior he always dies a hero's death. In *Atlakvida* his end is boldly and swiftly drawn:

> Then Hogni laughed
> as they cut to the heart
> of this bravest of heroes:
> he forgot to be sorry.

A man who could thus laugh in the face of death was greatly revered by the peoples to whom this legend was familiar. In the NL Hagen wins a great moral victory over Kriemhild: wounded and overcome by Dietrich, then bound and led to a dungeon, he resists Kriemhild's challenge to buy his life with the Nibelung treasure; on being shown Gunther's severed head his last words are: 'Now none knows of the treasure but God and I! You She-devil, it shall stay hidden from you forever!'[12] whereupon Kriemhild strikes off his head. Hogni in the Ths. falls after an honourable battle with Dietrich, refuses to be saved, and dies after living one more night during which he conceives the son who will cause Attila's death and thereby avenge the downfall of the Niflungs.

Moreover, Hagen possesses that highly-valued barbarian virtue, a *sense of honour regarding the keeping of oaths*. In *Skamma* Hogni's first reaction to Gunnar's suggestion that they slay Sigurd is that it is not seemly for them

> to break with a sword
> oaths that are sworn,
> oaths that are sworn
> and loyalties promised.

In the NL Hagen dies rather than break his oath sworn with the Burgundian kings not to reveal the treasure's hiding place as long as any of them still lived. Moreover, he is distinguished in the epic by his loyalty to Gunther and his devotion to furthering the interests of the Burgundian royal family. His reaction to Kriemhild's suggestion that he follow her and Siegfried to the Netherlands as their liegeman is one of indignation: the place of the men of Tronje (his birthplace) has always been in the service of the Burgundian kings.

Even Hagen's resentment of Siegfried in the NL is associated with his political loyalty to Gunther. 'Siegfried's pre-eminence irked Hagen. He could not suffer his king to be outshone.'[13] After Hagen has dealt Siegfried the fatal blow he says to the Burgundians, 'We shall not find many who will dare oppose us now. I am glad I have put an end to his supremacy.'[14]

Aside from these two basically heroic qualities, however, the German Hagen and the Nordic Hogni essentially part company. Since the Burgundian legend travelled North before events in Merovingian history had made their lasting mark on it, Gunnar has remained a great king with heroism untarnished and not a weakling leaning on an assistant who is the real tower of strength in the kingdom; therefore there was no room for a 'power-behind-the-throne' aspect of Hogni to develop. Moreover, the role of the 'villain', *i.e.* the agent of the Burgundian downfall, has in the Nordic tradition been unequivocally taken over by Atli who is motivated by power-lust and greed; virtually all of Hogni's 'traitor' aspect has thereby been eliminated, as well as any possibility of a Burgundian 'betrayer' blending with a corresponding Sigurd 'betrayer' in the Sigurd legend. Consequently Hogni[15] never attains the powerful stature enjoyed by the German Hagen. For one thing, Hogni has been absorbed into the family as Gunnar's younger brother[16] (probably as part of the tightening-up process deemed necessary for the relatively brief Eddic poems), which goes against the original German tradition by which all the names of family members must alliterate: Gibich, Gunther and so forth. Even his role as Gunnar's *confidant*, in which he appears consistently in all the sources, in the Scandinavian literature is subservient to the emphasis on family ties with Gunnar as king and head (as eldest brother) of the family; in two out of three of the important instances in which Gunnar requests Hogni's advice he ends up acting against his recommendations: he goes ahead with Sigurd's murder despite Hogni's observation that Brynhild in making the accusations against Sigurd is merely serving her own motives of hate, and he proceeds on the journey to Hunland, ignoring Hogni's warning of the treacherous nature of Atli's invitation. Only when Gunnar asks Hogni to dissuade Brynhild from committing suicide after Sigurd's death does he follow Hogni's advice to leave Brynhild alone as they will be better off without her. To be sure, the Hogni who steps forward to advise Gunnar is a wise and sensible figure, but never the cunning politician scheming for the king's or his own advancement, as would have been the case had his role as adviser logically developed from earlier sources and ultimately from historical models as an integral part of the character; instead – and the inconsistency of Hogni's adviser role with his place in the family as the king's younger brother testifies to this – what happened is that a remnant of that ancient role, from early sources in which the Hagen figure was an adviser but not a relative (or at least a more distant kinsman), has been transformed in the Sigurd legend into a mouthpiece of the old Scandinavian ethic, in order to remind the king (and indeed the poet's audience) of the necessity of *loyalty to oaths*, while in *Atlakvida* Hogni's urging of caution in accepting Atli's invitation serves to accentuate Gunnar's own heroism, in that he proceeds on the journey despite Hogni's warnings of the dangers that lie ahead.

Even Hogni's *ambivalent nature*, such an essential part of the mighty but enigmatic German character in its evolution from historical models, survives only as a remnant in the Nordic tradition: in *Atlakvida* Gunnar, challenged to reveal the whereabouts of the Nibelung treasure, demands that first Hogni should be killed. After this is done Gunnar says:

> My secret alone is the hiding place
> of the Niflung hoard, now Hogni is killed.
> While we both were alive I had my doubts;
> now I have none, since I alone live.

This has been interpreted as a suggestion that Gunnar did not fully trust Hogni.

It was events in Frankish history –fraternal strife, kings under the thumb of the Mayors of the Palace and so forth – which confirmed the German Hagen's evolution to the mighty figure known to us from the NL, which enshrines the Continental tradition in full bloom, and from *The Ring*. In contrast to the Scandinavian sources in which the family relationship is uppermost, the emphasis in the NL is on the political aspects of the Hagen-Gunther relationship: Hagen is the vassal and distant kinsman, as well as the closest confidant, of Gunther. But he is also more than this: he is no less than the *power behind the Burgundian throne*. He is extraordinarily well-informed about everything; the combination of this and his political acumen make him utterly indispensable to his weak, shifty king, and it is due to his superior knowledge and sagacity that he has managed to reach and retain his influential position at Gunther's court. It is Hagen who advises Gunther to ask for Siegfried's assistance in winning Brunhild; Hagen who conceives and carries out the plot against Siegfried; Hagen who causes the Nibelung treasure to be taken from Siegfried's widow and sunk in the Rhine; Hagen who fiercely opposes the trip to Hungary because he detects Kriemhild's treachery behind the invitation; and finally, Hagen who guides the Burgundians safely to Hungary because of his intimate familiarity with the roads.

Another characteristic with essentially political rather than personal implications is that of Hagen's *foreignness*, his being somehow different. In the NL his designation by the place-name of his origin, Hagen 'of Tronje', denotes him as a native of a different place from the one in which the present events are happening. The epithet 'of Tronje' or, to give the Ths. equivalent, 'of Troja', is believed to refer to the legendary Trojan ancestry of the Franks. Fredegar is the first author specifically to mention the Franks' supposed descent from the ancient Trojans; however, tales to this effect were quite current in fifth-century Gaul: 'Ammanius tells of fugitive Trojans settling in Gaul, and Ausonius sings of the heroes of the Trojan War.'[17]   In early forms of the lay of the Burgundians a Frank, as a non-Burgundian, would have been a foreigner, and given the contemporary interest in things Hellenic it would have been natural, even honorary, to refer to a Frank as a 'Trojan'.

Only the Ths. reflects the 'foreign' quality in terms of elfish origins: there Hogni is Gunnar's half-brother with an elf for a father. This situation raises the question of to what extent Hagen's 'foreignness' could have taken the form of partly supernatural origin in earlier forms of the legend, and although a digression to speculate on this is outside the scope of our discussion, it is nevertheless important to note that the representation of Hagen as different or foreign would not have been the primary purpose of such a supernatural birth or conception; rather, it would have been a way of acknowledging him as a person of note. It was not uncommon in the ancient world to attribute such unusual origin to outstanding figures; in Greek tradition, for example, Alexander the Great was supposed to have been fathered by a mysterious Egyptian who appeared as a prophet to lead the queen to believe that the god Ammon desired her,[18] while, closer to the time in which our legend was taking form, the chronicler Fredegar related how Meroveus, the hero who gave his name to the Frankish dynasty, was conceived when his mother was approached by a sea-beast while bathing in the sea.[19]   It is not unthinkable that a prototype of the Hagen figure in an early version of the Burgundian legend had such origins attributed to him in acknowledgement of his status as an important leader or hero, and the possibility becomes still more likely when one considers that such a connection with the supernatural could have been adduced to explain the source of his wisdom and knowledgeability; in fact some commentators have raised the suggestion that Hagen could have inherited 'second sight' from elfish forbears [20]   Hagen's connection with the supernatural has remained a consistent feature of the legend, from the Scandinavian *Atlamál* in which Hogni's wife relates to him her prophetic dreams regarding the tragic outcome of the Giukungs' visit to Atli, to the NL and Ths. in which en route to Etzel/Attila's court he encounters mermaids – 'water-fairies endowed with second sight'[21] – who foretell that none of the Burgundians will return alive from Hunland.

Hagen shares with his historical forbears the property that the very qualities which make him great also contain the potential for evil. Just as Stilicho and Aëtius, the mightiest men in the Roman Empire in their respective times, were suspected of using that power against Rome rather than in its interests; just as the Mayors of the Palace took advantage of their position in the service of the Merovingian kings gradually to usurp the royal power, so too is Hagen, in his position of trust as Gunther's confidant and adviser, capable of exercising that position in the king's interests or exploiting it for his own advancement, of choosing between what is best for the king and what will further his own ends. Here, then, is where Hagen's *ambivalence* enters the picture: the fact that, as with his historical forebear Aëtius, one sometimes does not know precisely which side he is on, and the suspicion that he will act out of self-interest while appearing to further the cause of his king. This characteristic survives in the mighty figure of the NL Hagen, and not unexpectedly is associated with that symbol of power, Siegfried's treasure. The poem refers repeatedly to Hagen's keen interest in the treasure which, after Siegfried's death, was Kriemhild's 'nuptial dower and thus it was hers by right'.[22]

> It was not for nothing that Hagen had desired it. In among the rest lay the rarest gem of all, a tiny wand of gold, and if any had found its secret he could have been lord of all mankind!

In the chapter describing how Kriemhild's family wrested the treasure from her by force Hagen at the King's suggestion sinks the entire treasure in the Rhine, 'imagining he would make use of it someday'.[23] But we are never told how he intends to make use of the treasure: for his own advancement or for the sake of his king? Is it possible that the NL Hagen, like Wagner's

Hagen, while for all intents and purposes appearing to act in the best interests of the Burgundian kingdom, would, if given the chance, seize the opportunity to gain power for himself? On the one hand we have that view which essentially blames Hagen for the Burgundian defeat on account of his failure to bow to Kriemhild's revenge for his murder of Siegfried; but on the other, Hagen's supposed 'coveting' of the treasure is never in any way connected with the slightest hint of disloyalty to Gunther. The interesting question here is, who is really guilty of ambivalence, Hagen or the NL poet? In terms of literary evolution the situation arises from the insufficient reconciliation of conflicting elements within the character. There are two types of conflicts: first, that between the early lays stressing the 'heroic' aspect of the Hagen figure and those stressing his traitorous disposition, and secondly, the incongruities arising when vestiges of the 'traitor' aspect remained with the Hagen character when the Attila figure essentially supplanted him in that role and Hagen's inimical qualities became minimised in favour of increasing and emphasising the solidarity among the Burgundian kin. Thus in the Hagen character we have a heroic figure, powerful and wise, who values honour and fidelity to oaths, and yet simultaneously one who exhibits traces of a treacherous character that would betray his kin to gain power and wealth. In terms of the NL specifically that enigmatic and mighty figure results from the poet's failure, as Hatto observes,[24] 'to relate Hagen at his greatness to Hagen at his depths'.

The most important aspect of the Hagen figure – his role in the slaying of Siegfried – has been left until last, for, aside from being that for which he is most readily identified in *The Ring*, it forms the primary link with the myth of Balder's death, the central aspect which stimulated in turn the absorption of many other elements of that myth into the Siegfried legend.

The parallels between the myth and the legend can be outlined as follows:

| BALDER-LOKI | SIEGFRIED-HAGEN |
|---|---|
| 1. Balder son of Odin | Sigurd descended from Odin (VS) |
| 2. Loki 'handsome, easy on the eyes' (Snorri) | Hagen's impressive appearance (NL); Hogni cuts a fine figure (Ths.) |
| 3. Loki not a full god; kinsman of Aesir, blood brother of Odin | Hagen kinsman of Gunther (NL); Hogni half-brother of Gunnar (Ths.) |
| 4. Loki helper, adviser to gods | Hagen helper, adviser to Gunther (NL, Ths.) |
| 5. Loki's duplicity, ambivalence:cannot be trusted; brings about end of Gods | Hagen's ambivalence: possible share in responsibility for Burgundian downfall (NL) |
| 6. Loki envies Balder because of his invulnerability | Hagen envies Siegfried because he outshines Gunther (NL) |
| 7. Balder impervious to all harm except for mistletoe which was thought too young to take oath not to harm him | Siegfried impervious to harm on all parts of body except spot between shoulder blades where a leaf fell and covered it while he was bathing in dragon's blood (NL) |
| 8. Loki tricks Frigg into revealing Balder's vulnerability | Hagen tricks Kriemhild into revealing Siegfried's vulnerable spot (NL) |
| 9. Balder killed by half-brother Höd with mistletoe which was too young to take part in oath not to harm him | Sigurd killed by brother-in-law Guttorm who was too young to take part in brotherhood oath sworn with him (Edda, VS) |
| 10. Balder killed through Loki's scheming | Siegfried/Sigurd killed by Hagen/Hogni through the latter's scheming (NL, Ths.) |
| 11. Balder's body burned on funeral pyre after his death | Sigurd's body burned on funeral pyre after his death (Edda, VS) |
| 12. Balder's wife dies of grief, is burned with him | Brynhild dies on Sigurd's funeral pyre (Edda, VS) |
| 13. Loki admits responsibility for Balder's death | Hagen admits killing Siegfried (NL) |

In some cases the originally historically-inspired

features of legend were stimulated, through a basic similarity, to still closer resemblance with the myth. Hagen's 'foreignness' is one example, an element with essentially historical origins whose retention in the legend must have been partially influenced by Loki's half-god status; other examples are Hagen's role as the wise and indispensable adviser to his king, and the suspicion of his sharing in the responsibility for the Burgundian downfall, since the survival of the 'traitorous' elements in Hagen's nature could well have been brought about through analogy with Loki's destructive role in the Ragnarök.

Still other parallels represent correspondences between myth and legend which were derived independently from but parallel to each other from the same sources; for instance, the old pagan religion survived considerably longer in the North than it did on the Continent, and some of its customs • – that of ceremonially consigning the bodies of great leaders (such as Viking chieftains) to the flames, for example – are immortalised as Scandinavian accretions on both the Balder myth and the Sigurd legend.

Most fascinating of all are those parallels between myth and legend which are too detailed, too unique to be attributable either to coincidence or to parallel incorporation from some common source, and which therefore represent definite incorporation from myth into legend. These revolve primarily around the slaying of the hero.

Snorri in his *Prose Edda* has left the following account of Balder's death:

> . . . Balder the Good had terrible dreams about his life. And when he told the Aesir about the dreams they held a conference at which it was agreed to guard Balder from all kinds of dangers; Frigg [Balder's mother] exacted oaths from fire and water, iron and all sorts of metals, stones, earth, trees, illnesses, four-footed animals, birds, poisons

and snakes, that they would not harm Balder. When this had been done Balder and the Aesir would play games in which he would stand up and all the others would shoot at him or strike him or throw stones at him; but whatever was done, it did not harm him, and all thought it was a great honour. But when Loki saw this he was filled with envy that Balder was not harmed. Disguised as a woman he visited Frigg . . . Frigg said: 'No weapon or tree shall harm Balder; I have exacted oaths from them all.' Then the woman asked: 'Have all objects sworn to spare Balder?' Frigg replied: 'West of Valhalla grows a twig called mistletoe; I thought it too young to demand an oath of it.' So the woman left; but Loki took up some mistletoe and went to where the gods were amusing themselves with Balder. But Höd was standing on the edge of the circle because he was blind. Loki said to him: 'Why do you not shoot at Balder?' He answered: 'Because I do not see where Balder is standing, and besides, I am weaponless.' Then Loki said to him: 'Still, do as the others and honour Balder! I shall show you where he stands. Shoot at him with this twig here!' Höd took the mistletoe and cast it at Balder as Loki directed him; it pierced Balder and he fell dead to the ground – and this is the greatest misfortune to have befallen gods and men.

As previously noted, the Nordic tradition lacks a prominent Sigurd-murderer, probably because the legend reached the North before a significant individual figure emerged in that role; there Sigurd is slain by the young Guttorm, who is put up to the deed by his older brothers Gunnar and Hogni. Only the German tradition knows the mighty Hagen, the king's indispensable adviser and military commander, as the murderer of Siegfried.[25] These differences affected the way in which the myth of Balder's death influenced the two forms of the legend. In Scandinavia primarily the Balder aspects were absorbed, with the emphasis on Sigurd as a reflection of the 'bleeding god'; the cunning and scheming Loki, on the other hand, never touched the Nordic Hogni but *only the German Hagen*. The only apparent reflection of Loki in the Nordic Sigurd tradition is that the slayer of Sigurd is not a full brother to Gunnar and Hogni but Giuki's stepson; this is recorded by Snorri and in the Eddic poem *Hyndla*.

Possibly this survives as an analogy with the half-god Loki, perhaps assisted by memories of Sigebert's assassin's having been a foreigner.

Thus while both the Nordic and the German traditions have absorbed elements from the myth for their accounts of the slaying of the hero, they appropriate different aspects of that myth: in the North half-brother becomes brother-in-law and the fatal weapon (mistletoe) has become the person who slew Sigurd (Guttorm), while in Germany the schemer ultimately responsible for Balder's murder (Loki) has become the actual killer of Siegfried (Hagen). The powerful schemer-as-murderer motif of the German version corresponds to the conception of Hagen as power behind the throne which developed on the Continent but did not reach the North: with the idea of the scheming murderer comes his power and insight – the clever Loki a suitable counterpart to the mighty, influential Hagen. In Scandinavia, on the other hand, that Sigurd had to be slain by someone who was out of the loyalty oaths (Guttorm had been too young to participate in them) was vital in the context of the Nordic ethical code, which held oath-breaking among the most grievous of offences.

In the German tradition Siegfried is invulnerable as a result of having bathed in the blood of the dragon whom he had slain. The motif of a hero completely invulnerable to harm except for one spot on his body occurs frequently in mythology and legend; the expression 'Achilles heel' for someone's vulnerable spot (physical or otherwise) echoes one example. That this motif was not absorbed into the Nordic Sigurd tradition is possibly due to its adoption in Germany (through Mediterranean influence?) after the Siegfried legend had travelled northwards. That it was taken into the German tradition is hardly remarkable in itself, but that the revelation through trickery of the hero's vulnerable spot was specifically taken over from the Balder myth makes for interesting speculation as to how and why this occurred.

In the NL it is Kriemhild who is tricked by Hagen. As part of the plot against Siegfried Gunther lies to everyone that war has been declared on him; hence all the men must prepare for battle. While this is happening Hagen goes to Kriemhild:

> 'Now tell me, Kriemhild, dear lady, what can I do for you with regard to your husband Siegfried? I should do it willingly, since there is none towards whom I am better disposed than you, ma'am.'
>
> 'I should not be afraid of anyone killing him in battle,' replied the noble lady, 'if only he would not let his rashness get the better of him. Apart from that, the good warrior would never come to harm.'
>
> 'My lady,' said Hagen, 'if you have any apprehension that a weapon might wound him tell me by what means I can prevent it, and I shall always guard him, riding or walking.'
>
> 'You and I are of one blood, dear Hagen, and I earnestly commend my beloved spouse to you to guard him.' Then she divulged some matters that had better been left alone. 'My husband is very brave and very strong,' she said. 'When he slew the dragon . . . the gallant knight bathed in its blood, as a result of which no weapon has pierced him in battle ever since . . . Now . . . I shall tell you, trusting utterly in you, where my dear husband can be harmed. When the hot blood flowed from the dragon's wound and the good knight was bathing in it, a broad leaf fell from the linden between his shoulder-blades. It is there that he can be wounded, and this is why I am so anxious.'
>
> 'Sew a little mark on his clothing so that I shall know where I must shield him in battle.' She fancied she was saving the hero, yet this was aimed at his death. [26]

The NL is the only extant source to contain such a revelation; was it the first? If so, then the poet's main reason for using it could have been its value as a literary device; instead of letting Hagen – who knows all about Siegfried's slaying of the dragon – know also about the hero's vulnerable spot from the beginning, the NL poet preserves the irony of an unwitting revelation of the hero's vulnerable spot by the person most anxious to protect him.

If, on the other hand, such a revelation also figured in

earlier, now lost forms of the legend, what was the motive for its inclusion? Probably this: The German tribes were Christianised several centuries before the North was; and because of the Germans' very adamant resistance to this conversion, the pressure upon them to renounce their pagan ways was most intense. Consequently no German sources exist to tell us about their old gods as such; thus one is tempted to advance the theory that the Germans preserved their pagan traditions in a disguised form, that is, by incorporating elements from their mythology into their heroic legends, in which case the absorption of features of the Balder myth into the Siegfried legend could be an example of such a disguise. Furthermore, this theory could help to explain why so many Loki attributes have found their way into the German Siegfried tradition despite the absence of any definite traces of a German mythological counterpart to the Loki who plays such a significant (and indeed not only in the Balder myth) role in Nordic mythology.

It would have been neither appropriate nor dramatically satisfying for Siegfried, Wagner's splendid hero, to meet his downfall in the manner of the Scandinavian sources, at the hands of a family consortium, slain by a minor figure who is urged on by his conspiring older brothers and then felled by his own victim before the latter expires; rather, such a powerful figure required an equally formidable antagonist, and therefore Wagner fashioned his mighty Hagen chiefly from the lordly and mighty vassal of the NL.

For Hagen to have been able to plan and execute his complicated intrigue against Siegfried he had to be in a powerful position of influence, and this he is, for like his forebear in the German epic he is Gunther's closest friend and most trusted adviser. Gunther acknowledges his dependence upon Hagen's knowledge and wisdom from their first entry on to the stage:

**Monuments to a heroic age.** 1. The Hermann Monument in the Teutoburg Forest, Detmold. 2. Ruins of the huge Roman amphitheatre at Xanten, possibly the site of St. Victor's martyrdom.

1

2

3

4

5

**The splendid hero.** 3. This mosaic, from a Roman country house in Germany, shows the brilliant, youthful sun god who is carried over the earth in his chariot. 4. A twelfth-century Nordic conception of Sigurd slaying Fafner. Detail from the carvings on the Hylestad Stave Church, Norway. 5. Jean Cox as Siegfried in *The Ring,* Hamburg State Opera.

KARL RIDDERBUSCH
als "HAGEN"
Staatsoper Hamburg

6

**The faces of Hagen.** 6. Karl Ridderbusch as Hagen in *The Ring*, Hamburg State Opera. 7. Hagen throws the Nibelung hoard into the Rhine at Worms. 8. Flavius Stilicho, from part of an ivory diptychon.

7

8

9

**Women in the hero's life.** 9. Thusnelda in the Triumphal Procession of the Roman conqueror Germanicus, painted by Carl von Piloty in the nineteenth century (Neue Pinakothek, Munich). 10. Detail from the seventh-century Franks Casket showing (far left) Sigurd consulting a seeress and (far right) the three Norns. 11. Votive stone to Dea Virtus: a warrior goddess from Cologne, a likely ancestor for the valkyries.

10

11

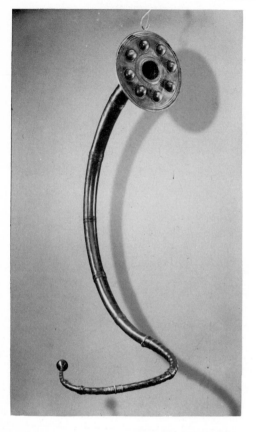

12

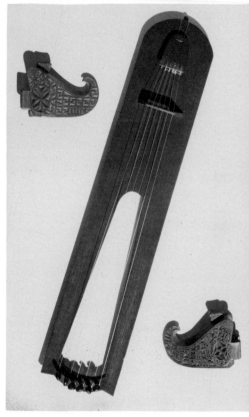

13

**Predecessors of the Wagnerian orchestra.** 12. Lur from Denmark: ancestor of the Wagner tuba? 13. Lyres such as this, from an Alamann singer's grave, accompanied recitations of heroic poems and songs.

> While I inherited the first-born's rights,
> wisdom was yours alone:
> half-brothers' rivalry was never better resolved.
> I only praise your counsel
> by asking you about my reputation.

In addition Hagen must, like his predecessors in history as well as in the NL and Ths., officiate in some sort of military capacity; this is suggested by his summoning of the vassals to prepare for Gunther's wedding in Act II: indeed, at first the vassals believe he is assembling them for battle. This scene is derived from similar ones in the above-mentioned epics, such as the one in the NL in which Hagen, having kept the night watch in Etzel's court, rouses all the Burgundian knights and exhorts them to don not their fine clothes, although they are going to church, but their shields, helmets and swords, for they will be compelled to fight the Huns that day.

Even this relationship with the vassals is something Hagen can eventually exploit for his own purposes: towards the end of *Götterdämmerung* we get another intriguing glimpse of the 'military' aspect of that relationship. After Hagen has admitted slaying Siegfried he claims the ring:

> Hagen: I have now earned the sacred right to booty:
> therefore I claim this ring.
> Gunther: Get back! What has fallen to me you shall never have.
> Hagen: You men, uphold my right!

Hagen bases his claim to the ring on the ancient legal concept of *Beuterecht*, the right of a person to keep the possessions of someone he has lawfully slain. His belief that the men would support his claim against Gunther's is traceable not to one of the literary sources for *The Ring* but to a significant historical phenomenon of the early Christian era. From about the second century A.D. the military was one of the most powerful classes in the Roman Empire, in that the selection of a new Emperor often fell to the soldiers of the Roman army;[27] in fact it was not unheard-of for troops to raise to the purple a much-admired commander to wrest the imperial power from a still-living but unpopular emperor. In this manner Julian the Apostate, while sub-ruler of Gaul, found Rome's highest responsibility thrust upon his shoulders, having been summoned to his window one midnight to hear from the troops under his command the proclamation, 'Julian Augustus!' A man who aspired to attain imperial rule in this way[28] needed to have confidence in the support of his troops against the reigning emperor. Hagen's belief that the vassals will support his claim to the ring is not unfounded if we recall in Act II how the hilarity and familiarity – even the joking and making of a pun on his name ('Hagedorn' = 'hawthorne') – with which the men greet his summons to the wedding preparations give way to the solemn clashing of spears as they sing, 'Heil dir, Gunther'. Just as the ever-present, obviously competent military commander could rely on the support of his soldiers against a distant emperor, so too was it not unreasonable for his legendary descendant, Hagen, who dealt with the Gibichung vassals on a daily basis and had close personal contact with them, to expect them to back his claim against Gunther.

Having thus given Hagen his extraordinary powers and installed him in a position of considerable influence at the Gibichung court enabled Wagner, for the sake of dramatic compression and in order to achieve a proper balance between the hero and his opponent, to extend considerably Hagen's influence over events: only in *The Ring* is the *entire* chain of events leading up to Siegfried's downfall the result of Hagen's machinations. Only the *Ring* Hagen could end his account to Gunther of Siegfried's history by wrenching the F-major tonality a semitone upwards into G-flat at the words 'den wünsch' ich Gutrun' zum Mann' ('I want him for Gutrune's husband') to express his determination to twist events

according to his own plans (ex. 1). It is through his
unlimited influence at the Gibichung court that he is able
to instigate the marriages between Siegfried and Gutrune,
and Gunther and Brünnhilde respectively, through taking
over functions which in the sources are distributed among
several characters. In the VS the following sequence of
events occurs:

Queen Grimhild (mother of the Giukungs) gives Sigurd a
  drink which causes him to forget about Brynhild;
Giuki and Gunnar give Gudrun to Sigurd in marriage;
Grimhild suggests to Gunnar that he go and woo Brynhild
  and that Sigurd should accompany him.

In *The Ring* it is Hagen who carries out all these functions
and, moreover, gives Siegfried an entirely new drink at the
end, one that restores his memory; however, here these
actions are not merely links in a chain of events as they are
in the saga, but interrelated with one another for the
purpose of serving Hagen's ambitions.[29] Because of his
knowledge of Siegfried and Brünnhilde's past together he
is only too well aware that the double marriage he is
arranging will result in Siegfried's falling directly into his
trap.

Further evidence of Hagen's power is his independence from Alberich. In *Siegfrieds Tod* Hagen was essentially the pawn of his father, but now in *Götterdämmerung* Wagner has ensured that he has ceased being that, whatever Alberich himself may believe. Hagen has no intention of handing over the ring to his father, and indeed, his ill-concealed resentment of Alberich, which surfaces in the Dream Scene in Act II, is a sufficiently compelling motive for Hagen to withhold from him the coveted talisman of power.

No precedent for the theme of father-betrayal as embodied in Hagen's relationship with Alberich exists in the literary sources, unless one counts the relationship in the Ths. between Hagen's son Aldrian and Attila, who acts as something of a foster-father to the boy. However, two striking historical parallels can be found in Gregory of Tours' account of the Franks. Mummolus, the retainer of King Guntram who figures as a Hagen forbear , rose to power through just such disloyalty to his father, Peonius, who was count of Auxerre. Hoping to have his appointment renewed Peonius sent gifts to Guntram through his son, but when Mummolus handed the gifts over he 'canvassed his own appointment to the countship: in effect he replaced the father whom he ought to have been supporting.'[30] The other example is Chloderic, son of King Sigebert the Lame, an ally of Clovis. Hoping himself for the support of Clovis if he were to succeed to the throne Chloderic had his father assassinated, then sent word to Clovis that he had taken over his father's kingdom and his treasure.

Here we have a most important instance of Wagner's reaching back beyond literature and legend to recorded history for his material. That Wagner specifically had the models of Mummolus and Chloderic in mind is indicated by the fact that he knew Gregory's *History*; moreover, Mummolus was singled out as an historical forbear of Hagen by Karl Wilhelm Göttling,[31] whose book Wagner had read. Compare the relevant portions of the texts of the 1848 and the final versions of the Dream Scene:

| SIEGFRIEDS TOD | GÖTTERDÄMMERUNG |
|---|---|
| Hagen: You shall have the ring! | Hagen: I will get the ring; rest assured of that! |
| Alberich: Do you swear that to me? | Alberich: Do you swear it to me, Hagen, my hero? |
| Hagen: You shall be free, and Lord of the Niblungs again! | Hagen: I have sworn it to myself; calm your fears! |

The irony of Hagen's last rejoinder is underlined by its musical setting (ex. 2): an ambivalent meaning behind his superficially innocent, C-flat-major reply to Alberich is suggested by the F pedal underneath it.[32] It is now Hagen who is in control, and the contrast between the excited, almost crazed Alberich – his speech characterised by wide intervallic leaps and jagged contours and accompanied by flurries of orchestral activity – and the cool, calculating Hagen, whose largely monotonic speech is scarcely accompanied at all, makes for effective drama.

ex. 2

There is an illuminating parallel with the Watch-Song, in Hagen's closing words: 'Though you think him lowly, yet you shall serve him: the Nibelung's son.' And indeed, logic and symmetry demand that no one but Siegfried's dark opponent himself, should he wrest the ring from the hero, enjoy the fruits of his victory.

What Wagner shows on stage and through the text he underlines and confirms in the music. The character of Hagen so overshadows and influences the events in *Götterdämmerung* that virtually all of the music in this work could be analysed in terms of Hagen's themes as basis of the musical structure. There is no room in this book for such a complete analysis, but some of the salient points should be mentioned. The most important musical device expressing Hagen's pervasive influence on the action consists of permutations of his tritone Leitmotiv (ex 3). In this particular context it is not so much the actual notes that matter but the contour and rhythm: one short note followed by a lower, sustained note. This aspect features in Act I Scene 1 in the Gibichung hall where the figuration has not yet attained the status of Leitmotiv *per se* but serves as a parameter of musical unity for the scene: its particular importance at this point is as an element in the themes representing the Gibichung family, and thus it depicts the family interrelationships among Gunther (ex. 4a), Gutrune (ex. 4b) and Hagen. Its later significance is adumbrated in the accompaniment to the question with which Hagen ends the disclosure of his plan to Gunther and Gutrune: 'Now tell me how you like Hagen's plan,' and it attains increasing prominence during and after the blood-brotherhood oath sworn between Gunther and Siegfried, before finally realising its definitive form as Hagen's Leitmotiv in the Watch-Song (ex. 3), which once and for all establishes Hagen's identity and his ambitions. Afterwards any appearance of a form of that

motif is identified as signifying Hagen's plan coming to fruition, especially as the derivations and related figures mostly occur as new stages of that plan materialise: for instance, the end of Act I when Brünnhilde has been overpowered by the disguised

Siegfried, and the end of Act II when the murder has been agreed upon. Even the dramatic chords which follow the actual slaying of Siegfried (ex. 5) and figure prominently in the Funeral Music are derived from the rhythmic idea of Hagen's motif.

ex. 5

In one important matter concerning Hagen Wagner took his cue from the Ths., and that was in making him an elf on his father's side. Wagner had several good reasons for taking this step. First of all, Hagen in *The Ring* is not the son of just any elf but of Alberich, the Nibelung who aspires to world domination: Wagner thereby achieved the Wotan-Siegfried/Alberich-Hagen symmetry that is so vital to his tetralogy. Moreover, Hagen's elfish descent explains his possession of knowledge and powers above those of an ordinary human, most significantly his complete knowledge of Siegfried's affairs, which enables him to conceive and execute the plot which will bring about the hero's downfall, and which is revealed to us in his account about the hero to Gunther in Act I that derives from the corresponding scene in the NL. Finally, Wagner preserves from the Ths. the association of that elfish descent with inferiority. In the saga Hogni suffers two denigrating references to his elfish origins. The first occurs during the conference held by Gunnar and his brothers regarding Attila's invitation to visit him. Hogni, recognising that this is a trap, urges against accepting the invitation, but Gunnar calls this view as bad as the advice that Hogni's father gave his mother, thus tauntingly referring to Hogni's elf father. Much later, during the battle in Hunland, Hogni challenges Dietrich to a final duel, during which Dietrich becomes angry at being resisted so long by a fairy's son. Possibly a survival from a racial or national slur on a Hagen prototype in an early lay, possibly, too, a reflection of the half-god status of Loki whose only friend was Odin, this notion of inferiority was appropriated by Wagner to give Hagen a motive for his hatred and resentment of his half-siblings and of Siegfried, the repressed enmity between the half-brothers surfacing in Gunther's remark, 'Shameless son of an elf', which derives from the above episodes in the Ths.

It was mentioned earlier that Wagner had to accentuate Hagen's negative qualities in order to make him a fitting opponent for Siegfried. Most important of these qualities is Hagen's *ambivalence*. If uncertainty exists about the extent to which the NL Hagen possesses this characteristic, such doubts are unequivocally dispelled with regard to his counterpart in *The Ring*. There Hagen's interest in Gunther's reputation is thoroughly a pretence, his influential position at the Gibichung court an advantage to be exploited for his own benefit. Moreover, Wagner increases Hagen's duplicity far beyond the suggestions of the sources by having him mislead Gunther and Gutrune about the function of the magic potion: they believe it was a love potion causing Siegfried to fall in love with Gutrune, while what it actually did was to destroy his memory of Brünnhilde. Just as the NL Hagen 'kept putting it to Gunther that if Siegfried were no more, Gunther would be lord of many kingdoms',[33] so too does Wagner's Hagen point out to Gunther that Siegfried's death

> brings you gain.
> Unheard-of power will be yours
> if you win from him the ring,
> which can be done only through his death.

The difference between epic and music-drama is that in the latter case we have no doubts that Hagen has no intention of sharing any power with Gunther once the ring is within reach.

Thus we see Hagen appearing on the surface to be working for Gunther's best interests and those of the Gibichung kingdom, but with the very means he uses in order ostensibly to serve the Gibichung interests – the arrangement of the marriages of Gunther and Gutrune to Brünnhilde and Siegfried respectively, and later Siegfried's murder, ostensibly in order to increase Gunther's powers and prestige through the acquisition of Siegfried's ring – he is really working to further his own ends.

What better way could there be to express this duplicity musically than through the harmonic implications of Hagen's tritone Leitmotiv? The music of scenes or passages in which Hagen's duplicity predominates – in which, particularly, the true meaning of what he says differs greatly from that which people infer – is based on the harmonic tension between these two notes which are as far apart in the scale as can be. One striking illustration occurs in the Dream Scene (ex. 6). The C-flat-major melody with which Hagen poses the question, 'The power of the immortals: who inherits it?' to Alberich is in itself straightforward and simple enough; but the sinister F-pedal lurking and crescendoing beneath Hagen's utterance – a tritone away from the C-flat tonality of Hagen's question – underlines the real meaning behind it; suspecting that Alberich has no intention whatever of sharing the power of the ring with him, he intends to obviate the problem by keeping the talisman for himself once he gets it.

ex. 6

Furthermore, almost the entire scene between Hagen and the vassals in Act II is based on derivations of this idea. As with the previous example the chief device is the harmonic tension arising from a pedal note clashing with tonality a tritone apart (ex. 7a), but occasionally the melody too is involved: for example, ex. 7b in which the F-sharp in the bass replaces the G which one would have expected.

ex. 7a

Nevertheless Wagner does raise Hagen above the status of a mere villain. He has not even neglected, for instance, to preserve some vestige of the original greatness of the character, through the masterly way in which Hagen proceeds to spin his web of intrigue and successively ensnare everyone into it. From beginning to end he is in full command of the situation, his principal weapons being the vainglory of Gunther his king and his own influential position at the latter's court. Furthermore, even in Wagner's Hagen can we recognise a sense of honour (if a somewhat perverse one) when we realise that he never lures anyone into misconceptions through deliberate lies;[34] if he has a tool in deception it is omission: he neglects to mention anything about Siegfried and Brünnhilde's past relationship at the appropriate points, and thereby lets people draw their own (erroneous) conclusions. He tells Gutrune that the drink would cause Siegfried to forget that he had ever seen or been near a woman before her, and this is the literal truth: he merely omits the fact that there was a specific woman in question.

Another aspect of Hagen's sense of honour, his regard for fidelity to oaths, is preserved from the sources in that, declining to participate in the blood-brotherhood oath sworn between Siegfried and Gunther, and therefore not bound to Siegfried by such an oath, he is free to carry out the revenge on him. Later, his reply to the men's shocked question, 'Hagen, what have you done?' after he has fatally wounded Siegfried – 'I have avenged perjury' – is technically correct, for Siegfried *has* had carnal knowledge of Brünnhilde: therefore his wooing of her for Gunther was not entirely honourable, especially in terms of what he swore on Hagen's spear.

Yet Wagner does not stop at preserving a trace of Hagen's ancient greatness. His true master-stroke is that, despite the necessity of emphasising Hagen's negative qualities, he does not fail to show us the other side of the coin. That other side is visible most tellingly in the Dream Scene. This nocturnal dialogue in which Hagen's father Alberich appears to him to inquire about his progress in acquiring the ring and to urge him on has no direct precedent in the sources, but elements of it can be traced to a fascinating variety of suggestive material in the literature:

1. Hagen's encounter and conversation with the mermaids en route to Hunland, who foretell the disastrous outcome of the journey (NL, Ths.); from this Wagner got the general idea of *Hagen's direct encounter with the supernatural.*

2. two scenes in the Ths., one depicting a nocturnal conversation between Grimhild and Attila in which she stirs up his greed for gold by referring to Sigurd's treasure which is being withheld from her by her brothers, and the other in which Hogni's son Aldrian quizzes Attila (at whose court he lives) about Sigurd's treasure, the whereabouts of which is seemingly known to no one. Attila describes the treasure to the youth; Aldrian asks how Attila would reward the person who could show him where the treasure is, and Attila replies that he would make him a powerful man in his kingdom. Aldrian then reveals that he knows the hiding place of the treasure (for Hogni before his death had handed over the keys to the

boy's mother, with instructions to pass them on to their son), and the two of them agree to ride alone to the spot. From these Wagner must have derived the notion of a *father-son dialogue about the treasure,* in which the father reveals information about it and incites his son to action, and the latter asks questions touching on power.

3. a lengthy passage in *Atlamál* in which Hogni's wife, Kostbera, recounts to Hogni the runes she has read and the dreams of warning she has had concerning his and Gunnar's ill fate if they undertake the journey to Atli. To each portion of the dream related by Kostbera Hogni counters with a rational explanation; the brothers are determined to go and he refuses to be put off by any dreams. The statement-response form of this dialogue, contrasting Kostbera's urgent warnings couched in her descriptions of her dreams with the answers of the cooly rational Hogni, could well have inspired the *statement (question)-reply form* of the *Götterdämmerung* Dream Scene in which the agitated voice of Alberich draws dispassionate response from Hagen. The following excerpts will illustrate the similarity:

| ATLAMÁL | WAGNER |
|---|---|
| Kostbera: | Alberich: |
| I saw your sheet | Sleeping, Hagen, my son? |
| burn up in the fire. | You sleep and hear him not |
| Up to the heavens | whom rest and sleep forsake? |
| high flames were reaching. | Hagen: |
| Hogni: | I hear you, crafty Nibelung, |
| Here is some linen | what have you now to tell my |
| in bad condition. | sleep? |
| It will be burnt soon. | Alberich: |
| That's what your dream | Remember the power you were |
| means. | born with, |
| Kostbera: | if you have the courage you |
| Saw a bear coming, | got from your mother at birth! |
| tearing great logs up, | Hagen: |
| waving his paws | If my mother gave me courage |
| so we were quite frightened; | I'll not thank her for it, |
| tight in his jaws | for she fell to your cunning. |
| he held us, all helpless, | Prematurely old, gaunt and pale, |

pow'rless to move;  
it was most alarming.  
Hogni:  
Strong winds will blow  
against us on the journey;  
storms from the east  
are foretold by these great  
bears.

I hate the happy,  
I never know joy!  
Alberich:  
Hagen, my son! Do hate the  
happy!  
Then you will love your sad and  
sorrowful father as you should.

When Wagner first sketched *Siegfrieds Tod* the main function of the Dream Scene was to provide the audience (as well as Hagen) with a narrative of foregoing events. It was one of many such narratives required, since the entire dramatised *Ring Cycle* had not yet been conceived, and consistent with this purpose was the scene's original format in which Alberich related the preceding events and Hagen's main contribution was to intersperse occasional questions which would elicit the story's continuation. By the time the final text of *Götterdämmerung* had been written the original purpose of the scene had become redundant, the events recounted therein having been actually dramatised in previous scenes or previous operas of the Cycle of which the original *Siegfrieds Tod* was now a part; instead, like other narrative passages in *The Ring* the Dream Scene now serves to present a specific character's (*i.e.* the narrator's, in this case Alberich's) point of view of the events being recounted. What makes the Dream Scene remarkable, however, is the light it throws on the personality of the character – *i.e.* Hagen – to whom the story is being told: that other side of the coin already alluded to. Thus it affords a gripping insight into the soul of a man with 'stifling neurotic difficulties to contend with, not of his own making, which give him a greater claim on our understanding than at first we thought',[35] a man who resents his chronically unhappy condition to such a degree that he wishes he had never been born. He sings of this to music derived from the Forswearal of Love theme: an ironic musical twist, for while Alberich was free to choose between love and power, his son has had the choice made for him, by his father who 'brought him up to hate'. In this connection it is significant that when working out the final version of the *Götterdämmerung* text Wagner added Hagen's Watch to the end of Scene 1; this Watch-Song, derived from night-watch scenes in the NL and Ths. depicting his fearless heroism and his capacity as 'Protector of the Nibelungs' (=Burgundians or Gibichungs, a role which even in *The Ring* he has not entirely relinquished), becomes an occasion for him to vent his resentment of his lot as a reaction to Gunther's slighting treatment of him: 'Though you think him lowly,' he sings, while the orchestral accompaniment is nothing if not the musical depiction of a fist clenched in seething anger. Hagen's motive for coveting the ring is thus not a purely evil one of greed for power and wealth, but a need to compensate for those qualities – the feeling of isolation, the inability to relate to other people or to enjoy life – that are his Nibelung heritage; indeed, in the strife between love and power Hagen must choose power, because he is incapable of experiencing love.

To encompass the downfall of the hero, thereby to win the ring – this is the central purpose for which Hagen has been begotten. Wagner takes over not only the deed itself from the mighty Lord Hagen of the NL[36] but also, for their dramatic value, many of the circumstances connected with it. One of the most significant events surrounding the murder plot is one derived not only from the NL but also from the Balder myth. This is Brünnhilde's disclosure to Hagen of Siegfried's vulnerable spot, which Wagner has fashioned from a combination of the NL version and the Balder myth. From the epic comes the role of the wife (as opposed to the mother) as the person who hands out the information, while from the myth comes the fact that the person revealing the hero's weak spot to the potential murderer is the person who originally arranged his protection. However, Wagner differs from both epic and myth in eliminating the trickery aspect, for which course of action he had various reasons. In the first place the only person who could have been thus tricked would have been Gutrune, which would have involved her in the action to a greater extent than Wagner would have wished, and anyway it would have been virtually impossible for her to possess such information after knowing Siegfried for such a short time (in the NL this episode occurs after Siegfried and Kriemhild have been married for quite a while). By allowing Brünnhilde to give Hagen the information Wagner gives her the chance to refer back to her valkyrie powers with which she protected Siegfried and thereby let the audience know how he acquired his invulnerability. Most importantly, however, Wagner preserves some aspect of the Nordic Brynhild's responsibility for the hero's murder by allowing Brünnhilde purposely to reveal his vulnerable spot to Hagen: the person who originally protected him now knowingly collaborates in the plot to murder him, a Wagnerian twist found in neither myth nor legend.

As in the NL Wagner's Hagen slays Siegfried during a hunt, then causes the corpse to be carried in to 'greet' his widow; as the Gibichungs lament the hero's death Hagen asks them ironically, 'Are you angry with me for it?' ('I do not know what you are grieving for,' says Hagen in the epic [37]), and finally, confronted by Gutrune's accusation, fiercely admits the deed; in the epic this does not occur until several years later when the Burgundians arrive at Etzel's court; Wagner, in order to tighten up the plot, places it almost immediately after Gutrune discovers the body.

But Wagner does infinitely more than preserve and adapt from his past heritage these external events. Rather, perceiving more keenly than many of the foremost philologists the significance of the Siegfried-Hagen legend as a reflection of the Balder-Loki myth, he makes Hagen's slaying of Siegfried the point at which history, myth and legend converge in a supreme expression of their essential unity.

In a footnote to *I Saw the World End* Deryck Cooke writes:

> In the final definitive prose-sketch for *The Young Siegfried* . . .
> [Wagner] made Wotan tell Erda . . . that 'the gods have been
> anxious about their end, ever since Baldur, the most gracious
> god, went under'. In the actual text of *The Young Siegfried* he
> removed the name Baldur, and replaced it with 'the gladdening
> one', but now linked the god with Siegfried by adding the words
> 'der im *Frieden Siege* schuf' . . . But in the final text for *Siegfried*
> itself, he removed the reference to the god altogether, having
> realised that the figure of Siegfried had absorbed him, as it were,
> and made him redundant. [38]

It did not matter, then, that 'it was clearly impossible for a
stage-work to move from one world to another – from Odin to
Siegfried, from Loki to Gunther and Hagen',[39] for Wagner saw
how unnecessary it was to do so: an historically-derived version
of the myth, in which human characters figure, could replace a
depiction of it in its purely mythical form, something made
possible once Wotan, through his demotion of Brünnhilde
from valkyrie to ordinary mortal woman, had handed over the
action, as it were, to his now fully human daughter and the
denizens of the human world she now inhabits.

While the Balder–*(Ring)*Siegfried relationship is one of total
absorption, of one-to-one correspondence, the matter of Loki,
on the other hand, is complicated by the presence of not one
but two Loki figures in *The Ring*: Loge and Hagen. This is a
very important innovation on Wagner's part. In none of the
sources do both Loki and Hogni or Hagen appear, except for
the VS, where Loki's fleeting appearance displays none of the
features which Hogni/Hagen otherwise shares with Loki. It is
the common features shared by Loge and Hagen that are of
such momentous significance in *The Ring*.

One would not expect a master like Wagner to make the
parallels between Loge and Hagen overly obvious; it is the
contrasts between them – Loge is as suave and charming as
Hagen is grim and forbidding – which perhaps strike us first;
but these contrasts are basically superficial, while the
similarities they mask are deep. Essentially they comprise the
two characters' assumption of the same functions but in
different contexts: both are helpers and advisers, indispensable

to the people who need them (the gods in Loge's case and the Gibichungs in Hagen's), and yet to those same people they both belong and yet do not belong: somehow they are considered inferior, outsiders, but are tolerated because of the advantages their wisdom has to offer. As Loge is only half a god, so Hagen is half a Gibichung; as the gods' grudging tolerance of Loge is expressed in Wotan's words:

> Of all the gods your only friend,
> I accepted you into this mistrusting group.
>
> (*Das Rheingold*, Scene 2)

so does Gunther's repressed contempt for his half-brother finally surface with the derisive epithet, 'Shameless son of an elf'. Both Loge and Hagen assume something of Loki's role of 'eternally plunging the gods into hot water, and quite often [getting] them out again with his crafty advice',[40] Loge chronically so – his advice to Wotan to get the Giants to build Valhalla by offering them Freia as payment, and to get them out of the resulting predicament his suggestion that they wrest the Nibelung hoard from Alberich as a substitute payment, is the one example dramatised in *The Ring* – while for Hagen it is exemplified in his arrangement of the marriages of Siegfried to Gutrune and Gunther to Brünnhilde and, when this goes 'wrong', his advice of Siegfried's murder as the only way to restore Brünnhilde's and Gunther's honour.

It must be noted that the different contexts in which the similarities between Loge and Hagen exist result from the events that have come to pass in the course of the Ring Cycle, between the time when Loge consorted with Wotan in *Das Rheingold* and Hagen enjoyed the favour of the Rhenish king in *Götterdämmerung*. The contrasts between Loge and Hagen therefore not only serve to veil the resemblances between them, they also reflect the mood of the Cycle at the time when each of the two characters appears: the bright and dashing Loge when the gods are young and full of optimism, the dark and sluggish Hagen when everything has (or will soon have) gone wrong and gods and heroes hurtle towards annihilation. This contrast within similarity is even expressed in the music, through variants of the Leitmotiv heard first in *Das Rheingold* Scene 1 in connection with the forswearal of love (ex. 8).

Both Loge and Hagen have a derivation of this motif associated with them, Loge because it figures prominently in his great monologue (*Das Rheingold*, Scene 2) in which he declares that the thing prized the most highly in the world is 'Weibes Wonne und Wert' – the joy and worth of a woman – and Hagen because it is frequently sung by him or played while he is singing. The variant associated with Loge, in major-key tonality and set in the tenor voice, expresses the attractiveness of the concept – love – whose virtues he extols (ex. 9), while for Hagen one prominent example of its use, in clouded harmony and darkly scored, should serve to illustrate its appropriateness for this sad and brooding character (ex. 10, bracket *a*).

The musical similarities and contrasts – in which the common theme is love, the difference is between the haves (of whom Loge sings) and the have-nots (of whom Hagen is one) – thus parallel and reflect the dramatic ones.

In fashioning his Loge figure Wagner has 'dispensed with the evil side of Loki's activities',[41] among which the most significant is the murder of Balder. And why? Quite simply, because he had Hagen to complete Loge's, and Loki's, tasks. Which is not to say that Hagen's murder of Siegfried in *The Ring* is a one-to-one absorption of Loki's mythical slaying of Balder in the sense of making that slaying redundant: rather, it is a continuation and indeed a *fulfilment* of the events which Loge was an agent in setting in motion in *Das Rheingold*. The relationship of Loki:Loge:Hagen is an essential key to understanding the structure of *The Ring*, because from that relationship arises not only the simple balance engendered by the presence of two parallel characters at opposite ends of the Cycle, but also the overarching dramatic symmetry generated by Hagen's role as completer of what Loge started. Taking both of these into account we can go so far as to state that Hagen is a reincarnation of Loge, the soul they share in common being that of Loki. Loge *as Loge* has not slain Balder or brought about the end of the gods; what he has done was to advise Wotan to snatch the Nibelung treasure from Alberich in order to pay the Giants, a fateful suggestion with consequences he did not foresee: that Wotan would not heed the request to return the ring to its rightful owners, the Rhinemaidens. Wotan's failure to comply with this, and the consequent unleashing of the ring into unknowing and incapable hands, has brought about the ensuing events of which Loge, through his advice first to offer the Giants Freia and then to replace her with Alberich's gold, was the inadvertent agent. Disgusted with the way things turned out, he decides to part from the company of the gods – only to return, at the end, as Hagen. Since intervening events will have caused the action to be handed over from the now impotent gods to men, the mythical chain of events begun earlier will reach their fulfilment in historico-legendary terms. *Thus Loge does not slay Balder: instead Hagen slays Siegfried.* Even his admission of the deed, a dramatic high point of *Götterdämmerung*, comes, via the NL, from Loki's taunting disclosure about Balder's death to Frigg in *Lokasenna*, an Eddic poem which Wagner certainly knew well because Wotan's admonition to Loge also owes its existence to it:[42]

| LOKASENNA | NL | WAGNER |
|---|---|---|
| (Loki:) | (Hagen:) | (Hagen:) |
| One thing more, Frigg, if you like to hear my evil runes: thanks to me, you will never see your son Balder return. | I am that same Hagen who slew Siegfried the doughty warrior! How dearly he had to pay for lady Kriemhild's maligning of fair Brunhild! There is no denying it, mighty Queen, I bear the entire guilt of your ruinous loss. | Yes, then! I was his slayer! I, Hagen, dealt the fatal blow! By my spear he was wasted, for he perjured himself on it. |

Hagen's act of slaying has as its consequences not only the historico-legendary equivalent of the mythical one – the destruction of the Gibichungs' Rhenish kingdom – but also the fatal mythical one itself: the downfall of the gods, the Ragnarök. In this way Wagner has highlighted and confirmed the mythical aspects of the legendary Hagen's origins, by letting his Hagen fulfil the function of his mythical as well as his historical and legendary forbears He confirms this further through the reference to the boar in *Götterdämmerung* Act III:

Hagen (to Gutrune): Victim of a wild boar,
Siegfried, your dead husband!

. . . . .

Gunther: Don't blame me, blame Hagen!
He is the accursed boar
who stabbed this noble man.

This equation of Hagen with a boar in connection with his slaying of Siegfried is extant only in the Ths., and for its full significance we must look to a wider context than that of Germanic myth and legend. In the Eastern and Mediterranean worlds there exist many stories of gods slain by boars or during boar hunts: Adonis and Attis are among such figures. The boar thus came to be regarded as the incarnation of the enemy of the gods.[43] Undoubtedly the reference to the boar in the Ths. could claim Eastern and Mediterranean origins, and it was because of its significance in this earlier context that Wagner took it into *The Ring*. Hagen as enemy of the gods: there is a shade of difference, however, between the attitude of the Nordic gods towards Loki and that of Wagner's Wotan towards Hagen. The Norse gods are well aware that Loki, perpetrator of evil, will destroy them at the Ragnarök but are powerless to do anything about it. The same is true of Wotan with respect to Hagen, but with the addition that he does not want to do anything about it: indeed, in accordance with Wagner's directive 'We must will what necessity imposes and ourselves bring it about'[44] he even welcomes, in *Die Walküre* Act II, the advent of Hagen as agent of fulfilment of that particular necessity:

> Only one thing more do I want,
> the end, the end!
>       . . . . .
> So receive my blessing, Nibelung son!
> What disgusts me deeply I give you as your inheritance,
> the empty splendour of divinity: let your envy greedily feed on it!

But what of the other significance of the boar: its function as fertility symbol in the Nordic mythology, animal of Freyr, god of plenty? Taken in conjunction with the outcome of the Ragnarök as foretold in *Völuspá*:

> Earth for the second time she sees arising
> out of the sea, fresh and green . . .
> Fields unsown shall grow and flourish,
> evils be banished, Balder return . . .
> A hall she sees standing, fairer than sunlight,
> thatched with gold, in Gimlé;
> there shall valiant lords have their dwelling,
> living forever in peace and joy.

138

can we conclude that Hagen also was inadvertently the agent for a better life? For surely, just as 'Earth for the second time arising', free of evil and yielding abundant harvests is what awaited the survivors of the Ragnarök, it must also be in store for the spectators (alas, all too often – in disregard of Wagner's directions – absent from the stage at the close of *Götterdämmerung*) present at the cataclysm with which the *Ring Cycle* ends.


## Notes

1. p. 18.

2. Thus it was natural that when, nearly decades later, Attila died during his nuptials with a German princess, popular imagination placed him at the scene of the Burgundian holocaust and claimed he had been slain to avenge the death of his bride's kin.

3. One feature of Hagen's youth that can be traced directly to Aëtius is his having spent time as a hostage at Etzel's court; this is mentioned retrospectively in the NL but treated in more detail in *Waltharius*, a tenth-century Latin poem unrelated to the Siegfried or Burgundian legends·but in which Hagen and Gunther appear. At the start of his military career Aëtius was sent by Stilicho as a hostage, first to the Gothic king Alarich and later to the Hun court, during which time he formed a close acquaintance with the young Attila.

4. p. 424.

5. *ibid.*, p 425.

6. p. 340.

7. Koestler, pp. 44f.

8. Davidson, pp. 169f.

9. Riehl, p. 149.

10. *History of the Franks*, p. 157, footnote 64.

11. pp. 288, 290-1.

12. p. 290.

13. p. 321.

14. p. 132.

15. *i.e.* only the pure Scandinavian Hogni, not the Ths. Hogni.

16. Here he is a full, not a half-brother.

17. Wallace-Hadrill, *The Long-haired Kings*, p. 80.

18. Wisniewski, pp. 242f.

19. ibid.

20. NL, p. 388.

21. NL, p. 193.

22. pp. 146f.

23. p. 149.

24. p. 323.

25. The Ths. as well as the NL is counted here, for, although written down in Scandinavia, the Ths. stems essentially from German traditions.

26. p. 121.

27. Gibbon discusses this thoroughly in his *Decline and Fall of the Roman Empire*.

28. Unlike Julian, who accepted this development with reluctance.

29. In the NL the two marriages are related as an exchange bargain but have nothing to do with Hagen; nor, in the absence of a past affair between Siegfried and Brunhild, is any magic potion necessary.

30. p. 236.

31. *Nibelungen und Gibelinen*. A German version of Gregory, *Gregor von Tours und seine Zeit* by Joh. Wilhelm Loebell (Leipzig, 1839) was in Wagner's Dresden library.

32. Compare the accompaniment to Hagen's question, 'Der Ewigen Macht: wer erbte sie?'

33. p. 117.

34. Surely a trait inherited from Loki, who never lies, but indeed is known as a teller of unpleasant truths.

35. Donington, p. 221.

36. As well as Hogni of the Ths.

37. p. 131.

38. p. 241.

39. *ibid.*, p. 129.

40. Snorri, quoted in Branston, p. 165.

41. Cooke, p. 241.

42. In *Lokasenna* it is Loki who reminds Odin:

> Remember, Odin, when long ago
> we blended our blood together;
> never would you have asked for ale
> unless it were brought for us both.

43. *Encylopedia of World Mythology*, p. 208.

44. Letter to August Röckel from Zurich, 25.1.1854.

# 6

# '. . .Worthy of Gibich's fame?'

If a powerful and mighty Hagen were to succeed in bringing down the strong, brave Siegfried, he would need certain tools to assist in putting his plan into action: above all, he would need a weak, dependent person whom he could manipulate to play an important role in the plot against Siegfried. Gunther was to be this tool.

Gunther, ruler of a kingdom on the Rhine, occupies a throne inherited from his father, Gibich. Gunther must be a leader of some renown, since Siegfried makes a point of calling on him in the course of his journey down the Rhine.

'Hoiho!Where are you bound, jolly hero?' Hagen calls out as Siegfried comes within sight of the Gibichung hall.

'To Gibich's stalwart son,' comes the reply. Then, as Siegfried enters the hall, he tells Gunther, 'I've heard your fame told far down the Rhine.'

Like many figures who derive from heroic poetry, however, Gunther has a fatal flaw; in his case it is an over-anxious concern for his power and reputation. His very first words in *Götterdämmerung* are a request to Hagen for a report on the state of his reputation up and down the Rhine; a little later the matter that most concerns him about the eventual marriages of himself and his sister Gutrune is that the marriages should increase the family's prestige. Gunther finally meets his downfall through Hagen's exploitation of this flaw.

The Gunther of legend is usually equated with Gundahari,

the Burgundian king who fell in the Hunnish onslaught of 436-437. This view, however, is a greatly oversimplified one, for it leaves several questions unanswered, the most vital one being that of how Gunther became involved with Siegfried. The fact is that the Gunther figure, rather like Hagen, represents in a sense a synthesis of characters from the two different traditions, Gundahari being the model for the Gunther of the Burgundian legend.

Gundahari, along with his father and brothers Gibica, Gundomaris and Gislaharius, are mentioned in the *Lex Burgundionum* written by their descendant King Gundobad, who reigned from Lyons between 480 and 516 and was the uncle-in-law of the Frankish King Clovis. Gundahari was no weak, indecisive ruler but strove to widen the boundaries of Burgundy and create a strong state. When he tried to extend his boundaries to the west he met with Roman resistance in the form of the armies of Aëtius, before the resounding defeat by the Huns in which 20,000 Burgundian warriors including Gundahari were killed.

Just as no individually distinguishable historical models for a Hagen figure of the Siegfried legend existed from the start, so is a similar situation true for the 'Siegfried' Gunther. In fact it may be assumed that both Hagen and Gunther, in the context of the Siegfried tradition, are later individualisations of what at the outset was a comparatively anonymous group of people: those relatives or in-laws who plotted and carried out the hero's murder. It was first · under the influence of events of the Merovingian period, when the incorporation of historical precedents for figures in the Siegfried legend (*e.g.* the Avar Chagan) occurred at approximately the same time as the merging of the two legends, that persons from that group of relatives or in-laws became differentiated into the individuals we now know as Hagen and Gunther. In Gunther's case this eventually meant the adulteration of the heroic qualities of the Burgundian king through the influence of historical models with less desirable features; Hatto[1] sums it up succinctly when he says that 'in Gunther's character there is enshrined a blend of perfidy, cowardice, cunning, finesse, and physical courage that strikes one as peculiarly Merovingian'. Again the strictly 'heroic' Gunnar of the Eddic poems on the fall of the Giukungs – *Atlakvida* and *Atlamál* – points to the possibility of the Burgundian legend's having travelled to the North before the merger with the Siegfried legend, thus before the 'contamination' of the heroic Gunther by later, weaker figures; indeed, even the Gunnar of the Sigurd poems cannot be claimed to be weak, his major flaw being his ambition to seize all the gold and power shared by himself and Sigurd.

We have already seen how the fusion of the legends of the Burgundians and of Siegfried arose from their sharing of such important themes as the lust for treasure and power. *King Guntram of Burgundy* (died 593), brother of Sigebert, is one Merovingian figure who had a major influence on our legend and especially on the fusion of the two traditions. The similarity of Guntram's name to that of the original Burgundian king Gundahari, and his connection with the themes of internal strife and power-lust, were factors in the merger. It was with the entry of Guntram onto the scene that Siegfried's hostile relatives acquired their specific identities, becoming his blood-brother/brother-in-law and equated with the Burgundian king and his kinsman Hagen. At this time too the political aspects of the chief characters' legendary relationships were founded: the various treaties and arrangements made among the Merovingian royal family members are thus reflected in literature:

VS: upon his marriage to Gudrun Sigurd holds *dominion as a prince of the land* of Gunnar;

NL: the Burgundian kings tell Siegfried they mean to *share with him the lands and castles* they possess as sovereigns;

Ths.: upon marriage to Grimhild Sigurd receives half of Gunnar's kingdom for dowry, thereby *becoming co-ruler with Gunnar* of Werniza (Worms);

*Götterdämmering* Act I:

Gunther: O hero, greet with joy the home of my father.
Wherever you walk, whatever you see,
regard as your own:
yours is my inheritance, my land and my people:
my body, support my oath!
I offer myself as your man.

Siegfried: Neither land nor people can I offer,
nor father's house or estate:
all I inherited was my own body;
while I live I use it up.
I have only a sword which I forged myself:
my sword, support my oath!
With myself I offer it to our alliance.

Just as Merovingian fraternal strife reinforced similar tendencies in the legend, so too, paradoxically, did King Guntram's behaviour contribute to the concept of family loyalty in the legend. Because Guntram ruled over the farthest-removed part of the Merovingian realm he felt insecure and thus stressed family ties. 'Guntram was forever exhorting his relatives to unity, and patching up vendettas where he could.'[2] In literature this survives in Gunther's initial loyalty to Siegfried, established by their swearing of brotherhood oaths.

No other individual Merovingian king stands out as a Gunther model to compare with Guntram. It was in succeeding generations that the decline of the dynasty set in and the royal authority was gradually usurped by the Mayors of the Palace. People in the decades immediately following the deposition of Childeric III thought of the last Merovingian kings as exceedingly weak,[3] and this (possibly exaggerated) view of the late Merovingians' failings coloured off on the Gunther figure, thereby completing the picture of the dependent, vacillating Burgundian monarch as he appears in the NL and in the *Ring Cycle*.

The sources do not exclusively depict Gunther in the unfavourable lights of dependence and prestige-concern which shine on Gunther of *The Ring*. As with Hagen, Gunther's varied evolutionary history resulted in the emphasis of first one, then another set of characteristics. The early traditions in which the different evolutionary processes took root can be summed up in the statement that with Gunther, as with Hagen, a significant factor in his character formation was the grafting of a figure connected with the hero's murder and the seizing of his treasure in the Siegfried tradition on to the heroic king of the Burgundian legend. When the qualities of the figure of one tradition were at variance with those of the character of the other tradition, the inconsistencies in the personality arose.

The Gunnar (perhaps one should even say 'Gunnars') of the Eddic poems offers a good illustration of the character's contrasting personal traits. The unsullied heroism of the original historical model, the Burgundian king Gundahari, survives only in the Gunnar of the Atli poems. *Atlakvida* and *Atlamál* depict Gunnar as a great warrior king. An important element in heroic poetry is the refusal to be a passive victim of overwhelming fate. Thus, though he may ask Hogni's counsel, in the end it is Gunnar himself who ultimately makes the fateful decision to undertake the treacherous journey to Atli despite all the warnings, because to shrink from the dangers he knows he must face would not be fitting. He bravely dies a hero's death and his last words are certainly among the highlights of Eddic poetry:

> Now shall the Rhine rule over the treasure,
> the strife-causing metal, the Niflung inheritance.
> Let the rings of the Gauls gleam in billowing water
> rather than shine on the arms of Hun offspring.

A feature shared by the Gunnar of the Atli and the Sigurd poems is his role as the 'high king' who, although he asks Hogni's advice, ultimately makes all the decisions himself. However, the Gunnar of the Sigurd poems, in contrast to his counterpart in the Atli poems, has been contaminated by the less desirable features of such historical personages as the Roman Emperors who occupied their thrones as figureheads

while the military commanders did the real work of defending,
maintaining and expanding the Empire, and the late,
increasingly weak Merovingian kings who came ever more
under the thumb of their Palace Stewards, until the last one
was quietly deposed. He takes a wife (Brynhild) won for him by
another man (Sigurd) and, prompted by lust for power and
wealth, has the hero murdered. His desire for power and
wealth, and his concern for his reputation, are evident in his
reaction to Brynhild's urging to have Sigurd murdered; she
stirs up his desire to take possession of Sigurd's treasure and
thus assume the power that is Sigurd's, and threatens to leave
Gunnar if her wishes are not complied with:

> You, O Gunnar, stand to lose
> the lands I own and me myself:
> life holds no joy for me living with you.
> I will return to the land of my father,
> back to my friends, back to my kinsmen;
> there shall I sit and spend my time sleeping
> if you slay not Sigurd the mighty,
> taking his place as greatest of princes.          *(Skamma)*

This threat also excites Gunnar's concern about what people
would think if Brynhild were to leave him, as well as about
losing her inheritance:

> Gunnar weighed the matter with care;
> it was not a normal thing
> for a queen to leave throne and husband.
>
> [Gunnar then puts it to Hogni:]
> Brynhild alone I value most highly;
> Budli's daughter is fairest of women.
> Gladly will I lay down my life
> rather than forfeit that maiden's treasures.
> Shall we slay Sigurd to better our lot?
> Good it is to control the Rhine's metal
> and peacefully to enjoy
> the security brought by such wealth.          *(Skamma)*

Heedless of Hogni's subsequent observations about the
dishonour involved in breaking their oaths sworn with Sigurd,
Gunnar persists with the plan to have Sigurd murdered,
deciding that they should get Guttorm to do it since he had not

been involved in the oaths. Thus Gunnar's decisiveness, an admirable quality in the Atli poems, here has negative consequences: his desire for power and wealth sways him to follow Brynhild's exhortations. In *Brot* he does so without bothering to hear Sigurd's version of Brynhild's accusation against him; in *Skamma* there are no such accusations, only Brynhild's threats and admonitions to which he gives in.

The VS juxtaposes the two sides of Gunnar by combining elements from different Eddic poems; his betrayal of Sigurd is somewhat mitigated by the use of the older version in which Gunnar is deceived into believing that Sigurd has betrayed him.

The NL, on the other hand, tends to emphasise Gunther's negative qualities – the weakness and dependence inherited from the Roman and Merovingian historical forbears – as if the epic itself evolved from sources that did likewise. The negative features of the Gunnar of the Sigurd poems pervade the entire character of the NL Gunther: unable or unwilling to assume responsibility for any important decision, he relies completely upon his vassal and kinsman Hagen for any formulation of policy and to implement important decisions. Hatto has thus accurately summed up the relationship between Gunther and Hagen:

> Gunther is a king in name but little else . . . Before the poem begins he has already learnt to rely on Hagen. Confronted with the imponderable threat of young Siegfried . . . he is sorry that Hagen stays silent so long, and . . . when Hagen does speak up he is 'Hagen the strong'. On such strong men can weak kings lean. [4]

The only thing Gunther undertakes of his own accord is to take Brunhild – a woman far above his own power to attain – as wife, for which he again requires outside assistance, in this case Siegfried's. While in the Nordic sources Sigurd's assistance is required and given on the spur of the moment, when he and the Giukungs discover that only Grane, with Sigurd on her back, can ride through the flames that loom up before them, in the NL Siegfried's cooperation, and the attendant deception, are planned in advance.

One feature which Gunther shares with his more heroic Nordic counterparts is the manner of his death, for at the end even the NL's vacillating Burgundian monarch, his ancient barbarian 'genes' at last coming to the surface, finally appears in a favourable light at the crucial moment by refusing to buy his life at the expense of Hagen's.

It is obvious that the identification of the *Ring* Gunther with the historical King Gundahari is not merely an oversimplification, but indeed downright misleading. Any trace of the heroism of the original Burgundian warrior king has been completely obliterated, Wagner's Gunther deriving exclusively, via the NL, from the historical 'weaklings' mentioned above and from the Merovingian King Guntram, Sigebert's brother. Even the latter's strong sense of family bonds, in itself a favourable or at least a neutral quality, has in Gunther degenerated to an obsession with continuing the family prestige established by his father Gibich.

Gunther's concern for his reputation, and his willingness to let others do the work of maintaining and increasing that reputation, are inherited from the NL Gunther and in turn are a legacy of the Roman Emperors who officially (but in no other sense) stood over such illustrious commanders and statesmen as Stilicho and Aëtius.

Gunther's theme music, a feeble travesty of a royal fanfare, is an apt musical portrayal of the weak, figurehead king; significantly, it is first heard accompanying his query to Hagen about the state of his reputation. Its oscillation between major and minor reflects Gunther's shifty character while the prevalent dotted-quaver rhythm suggests his vain officiousness (ex. 11). This theme differs from the true Leitmotivs in its relatively static nature, its lack of open-endedness. When Siegfried appears in Gunther's guise to woo Brünnhilde a

ex. 11

two-measure compact version of the theme is heard, always juxtaposed with the Tarnhelm motive, the quasi-modal tonality of this extract underlining the other-worldly aura of Brünnhilde's (seemingly) ghostly visitor (ex. 12).

ex. 12

It was Gunther's role in *The Ring* as Hagen's tool that determined Wagner's heavy use of the NL for his Gunther, for to fill that role Gunther's complete dependence upon Hagen is necessary to the plot. Indeed, while the lengthy epic elaborates more extensively upon this aspect of the Gunther-Hagen relationship, Wagner, limited by practical considerations of time, intensifies it by increasing the degree of Gunther's reliance upon Hagen. Thus, for example, in the NL Gunther himself makes the decision to woo Brunhild, but in *The Ring* Hagen makes the decision for Gunther. In the NL Gunther attempts to arbitrate in the quarrel between Brunhild and Kriemhild; in *The Ring*, when the altercation ensues upon Brünnhilde's arrival at the Gibichung shore of the Rhine, Gunther, totally crushed, can only cry, 'Help, Hagen! Help save my honour!'

The hypocrisy inherent in Gunther's 'prestige' weakness was developed by Wagner in the course of the fashioning of his text. In the prose sketch of 1848 Gunther claims the ring after Siegfried's death by reason of his marriage with Brünnhilde; this claim – 'Shameless son of an elf, the ring is mine, since it was intended for me by Brünnhilde: you all heard it!' – is based on Brünnhilde's earlier challenge to Gunther to demand the ring from Siegfried: for when Brünnhilde had seen the ring on Siegfried's finger which she believed Gunther to have wrested from her on the mountain she demanded the ring from Siegfried because it belonged not to him but to Gunther who got it from her (or so she believes). In contrast, however, stands the final text in which Gunther's claim to the ring is based on its being Gutrune's inheritance, and here is where the hypocrisy rears its head as we can be sure that Gunther has no intention of giving the ring over to his sister as a memento of Siegfried. Moreover, this indicates how even during the working-out of his text subsequent to the original sketch Wagner must have repeatedly gone back to consult his sources, for the final version is consistent with the hypocrisy of the NL Gunther and in particular with the Burgundian kings' taking of the treasure from Kriemhild on the pretext of safe-keeping.

One exception to Wagner's almost exclusive use of the NL for his Gunther occurs in the scene in which Siegfried first enters the Gibichung hall. The substance of this scene was based on the opening of the Eddic poem *Gripisspá*, in which Sigurd meets the great king and wise man Griper. One notable feature which this passage in *Götterdämmerung* shares with *Gripisspá* is that in both cases the hero has been expected by the person whom he has come to visit. The corresponding parts of the Eddic poem and of Wagner's text are set out below for the sake of comparison; the parallels between Griper and Gunther, and Geiter and Hagen, are obvious:

GRIPISSPÁ

Griper was the son of Öylime and the brother of Hjordis. He ruled many kingdoms and was the wisest of all men, and moveover, a seer.

Once Sigurd rode out alone and came to Griper's hall. It was easy to recognise Sigurd. Outside the hall he began to converse with a man named Geiter. Sigurd greeted him, requested information from him and asked:

'Who lives in this fortress?
What do warriors name him?'
Geiter said:
'Griper is the name of the ruler,
who rules here over land and warriors.'
Sigurd said:
'Is the wise king home?
Will he grant me an audience?
An unknown man is entitled to have his say.
I want to meet Griper immediately.'
Geiter said:
'Then the happy king shall ask
who it is who seeks him.'
Sigurd said:
'I am called Sigurd, son of Sigmund,
Hjordis is the name of the prince's mother.'

Then Geiter went to tell Griper:
'An unknown man has come.
He has an impressive appearance.
He wants now to meet you, King.'

The Lord of Warriors left the hall
to greet the newly-arrived prince:
'Be welcome, although you have taken a long time!
Go and look after Grane, Geiter!'

## GÖTTERDÄMMERUNG

Gunther:   The horncall comes from the Rhine .

Hagen:   A hero and horse in a small boat!
It is he who cheerfully plays the horn!
With easy-going strokes, as if his hands were idle,
he steers the boat fast against the current:
Only he who slew the dragon
can boast such vigorous strength in the swing of the
    oar.
It is Siegfried, certainly no one else!

Gunther:   Is he driving by?

Hagen:   Hoiho! Where are you going, jolly hero?

Siegfried:   To Gibich's stalwart son.

Hagen:   I invite you to his hall. Here! Moor here.
Hail! Hail, Siegfried, dear hero!

| | |
|---|---|
| Siegfried | Which is Gibich's son? |
| Gunther: | It is I, Gunther, whom you seek. |
| Siegfried: | I have heard about you far down the Rhine. Now fight with me or be my friend! |
| Gunther: | Forget the fighting! Welcome! |
| Siegfried: | Where shall I put my horse? |
| Hagen: | I will take care of him. |

An original contribution of Wagner has been to make Gunther's prestige obsession the flaw which Hagen exploits for his own ends: it is the means by which Gunther becomes a pawn in Hagen's deadly game. First, he is unwittingly led into the trap of entering the prestige marriage with Brünnhilde, and consenting to his sister's prestige marriage with Siegfried, unaware that Siegfried and Brünnhilde have already sworn oaths of betrothal to each other. Secondly, he agrees to the murder of Siegfried after Hagen points out to him that untold riches and power would be gained by him if Siegfried were removed. Even the music reflects Gunther's role as Hagen's pawn: except for the scene in which Siegfried appears in Gunther's guise the latter's theme is used only when he is actually present, a fact which shows what an ineffectual character he is, completely without influence on anything. After its culmination in the impressive wedding music for Gunther and Brünnhilde – only here do we get a fleeting glimpse of a glorious barbarian king, for perhaps Arminius or Gundahari would have had such nuptial music for themselves had the Wagnerian orchestra been at their disposal – the theme is never heard again, Gunther's purpose in Hagen's scheme – to get the ring within Hagen's reach – having now been fulfilled.

Another Wagnerian contribution – not entirely original but one in which Wagner reached beyond the extant literary sources to legend – was to allow Hagen, the half-brother and adviser, to murder Gunther; Wagner thus returned to an ancient, probably unwritten form of the legend – *i.e.* the very

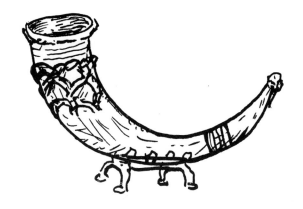

'Drink, Gunther,  drink':

German drinking  horn from the Migration Period.

early 'inside-job' concept of the Burgundians' betrayal and
defeat – thereby restoring to Hagen the role of his original
legendary predecessors which later became attached to the
Attila figure.

In still a further matter involving Gunther's death Wagner
reached back beyond legend to history. All the sources depict
Gunther dying heroically; but if we focus – as indeed Wagner
did, if only indirectly – on Gunther's 'Frankish' ancestry rather
than his descent from the brave Gundahari, then his
ignominious end in *Götterdämmerung* can be seen to reflect
the quiet deposition of the effete Childeric III, the last
Merovingian king, in favour of Pepin.

It is noteworthy, moreover, that Wagner departs from the
sources in that in effect he divorces Gunther's death from the
downfall of the House of Gibich. In the legend (as well as in
history, in the case of Gundahari) the death of the king and the

defeat of his entire nation are one and the same event; in *The Ring*, however, the cataclysmic destruction of the Gibichung Hall on the Rhine reflects in spirit the holocaust of the Burgundian defeat, only here the king is already gone, having died the disgraceful death of a greedy coward. Having fashioned a 'Frankish' Gunther, Wagner logically and consistently lets him meet a 'Frankish' end.

**Notes**

1.   NL, p. 326.

2.   Wallace-Hadrill, *The Long-haired Kings*, p. 199.

3.   *cf.* Einhard's Life of Charlemagne, quoted in *The Long-haired Kings*, p. 231f.

4.   NL, p. 324.

# 7

# The Nibelungs and Their Treasure

The Nibelung hoard and, above all, the ring fashioned by Alberich from the Rhine gold are in a sense the central 'character' of the *Ring Cycle*, for one of the main themes of the tetralogy is the struggle between Wotan and Alberich for possession of the ring, and the fate of those into whose hands it finds its way.

Properly speaking, in Wagner's case a distinction exists between the ring and the treasure, both because of their respective different origins and because of a slight difference in their symbolic functions: the ring is the primary symbol – indeed, the agent – of power, while the treasure is secondarily the symbol in that it reflects or recalls the power (imparted by the ring) necessary to have caused it to be amassed.[1]

The salient features of the Nibelung hoard with regard to its historico-legendary significance are, firstly, the importance of the treasure and the ring as a symbol or accoutrement of earthly power, and secondly, its origin with a Nibelung and the fact that a (son of a) Nibelung – along with his half-siblings the Gibichungs – seeks to regain it; the latter is a vital element to the dramatic balance of the *Ring* tetralogy.

Just as the Nibelung hoard and ring qualify as the central 'character' of the *Ring Cycle*, so too do wealth, and the power it signifies, constitute the element that runs like a red thread through the historical events which form the basis for Wagner's literary sources.

The Nibelung treasure, like some of the human figures in the legend, represents a synthesis of elements from the two originally separate halves of the legend: Siegfried's treasure and the Burgundian treasure. In the extant literary sources Siegfried's treasure is comprised not only of the dragon's hoard but also of his wife's dowry and wealth won from war campaigns; among the historical models for such a treasure are King Sigebert's own wealth and Brunechild's dowry. Yet even here we stand on post-Merovingian ground, at a point of time beyond the fusion of the two legends. As we narrow our focus to the pure Siegfried legend the striking fact about the hero's treasure is that it was *gained in a contest* or struggle. The role of Arminius in the shaping of this aspect of the legend must not be overlooked, for in his battle against the legions of Varus Arminius won not a minor campaign but a major victory, one with significant implications for the subsequent course of European history and one, moreover, in which the young chieftain and his warriors *captured the three standards* of the Roman legions – 'an almost unbearable humiliation for the Empire'.[2] Such standards, symbols of a resounding victory, were indeed in their own right a treasure; thus it was completely natural that this victory of Arminius, in the course of its absorption into legend, assumed the timeless mythical form of the hero's winning of a treasure (*cf.* Chapter Two).

The association of a treasure with a kingdom was common among the nations of the Migration Period. The hoard of the Goths was discovered in 1837 in Rumania, the so-called Pietroassa Treasure, one of the most splendid of its kind. In 1858 a Spanish farmer found a treasure which included the crown jewels of the Visigothic kings, whose capital in the seventh century was Toledo. Three of the golden crowns bore the names of Visigoth rulers: Swinthila, Rekkeswinth and Sonnika.[3] In both cases the treasures had been buried by their owners in order to prevent theft by enemies, the Gothic hoard probably by King Athanarich in 376 when his kingdom broke up and the Goths moved westwards, while the Visigoths sought to conceal their jewels from the invading Arabs. This phenomenon, of which these two are by no means isolated instances, is reflected in legend in that the Nibelung treasure is sunken into the Rhine (*Edda*, NL) or concealed in a mountain (Ths.), as well as hidden by Fafner in a cave in *The Ring*.

We have already noted the role of treasure as an accoutrement of power in the Merovingian kingdom; if we trace the history of the Burgundians we shall see how they, too, would have come to have a treasure asociated with them once they were immortalised in legend.

The 'glorious race' of the Burgundians, migrating to the Continent from the island of Bornholm before the birth of Christ, eventually settled along the Rhine and there established a kingdom in 406 A.D. Some thirty years later the Burgundians were ruled by King Gundahari, who with his family is named in the *Lex Burgundionum* of King Gundobad. Gundahari's disastrous encounter with the Huns followed upon his attempt to invade the Roman province Belgica I, the capital of which was Trier.[4] The survivors of the defeat were resettled by Aëtius in Sapaudia (Savoy), on the Lake of Geneva and on the Rhone, where they maintained an independent kingdom until its overthrow by the Franks in 534.

Traditionally the city of Worms has been held to have been the capital of this Burgundian realm[5] but it is not known for certain whether this is historically correct. To be sure, even from pre-Roman times Worms was a very important town because of its Rhine crossing, and the commercial significance of this location made the town prosperous. Therefore it was quite natural for stories about treasures to spring up in connection with the inhabitants of that area. It is often maintained, too, that the red rock in the Worms region, which causes a shimmering gold effect in the Rhine, gave rise to tales of a treasure sunken in the river.

Another town on the Rhine associated with the

Burgundians, known to have been inhabited first by them and then by the Franks, was Neuss, near present-day Düsseldorf. In ancient sources Neuss has been variously referred to as Novesium (Tacitus), Nivisium (Ammianus) and Niusa (= Nivisa: Gregory of Tours), the root *niv-* or *nov-* etymologically pertaining to a place located close to water. Other such towns whose names have this root are the modern Noyon sur Aisne (Noviomum),[6] and the English town of Chichester, which in Roman times bore the name Noviomagus. In the old Frankish tongue an inhabitant of Neuss was called a Nivilinc, Nivulinc or Novilinc, depending on the form of the city's name in use.[7] Such linguistic findings have led to the theory that 'Nibelung' or a form of the name was in fact the dynastic name of the Burgundian royal family, just as the Ostrogothic royal family was called Amelung.[8] As a first and last proper name the name 'Nibelung' and its variants have been traced back in history and found throughout Europe, especially among the Rhenish Franks[9] and surrounding areas; it has appeared as early as the fifth century in the area of the Burgundian settlement.

Therefore that the Burgundians are sometimes called Nibelungs in the literature is not a result of a mistake or confusion[10] but indeed firmly based in history. In the *Edda* it implies a dynastic name: Brynhild uses the expression 'House of the Nibelungs' in *Brot*; Gudrun calls her brothers the Nibelungs in *Gudrunarhvöt*. Most important is the appearance of the term in *Atlakvida*; the age of this poem – the version handed down to us is believed to date from around 870 [11] – testifies to the antiquity of the association of the name 'Nibelungs' with the Burgundians or Giukungs/Gibichungs. There several of the references to the Nibelungs involve the Nibelung treasure: before embarking on the journey to Atli Gunnar resolves:

> The wealth [12] of the Niflungs shall fall to the wolves,
> grim and grey, if Gunnar be lost.

Later, when refusing to disclose the treasure's hiding place he declares:

My secret alone is the hiding place
of the Niflung hoard, now Hogni is killed . . .
Now shall the Rhine rule over the treasure,
the strife-causing metal, the Niflung inheritance . . .[13]

It must be remembered that *Atlakvida* nowhere implies any connection with the Sigurd legend; the treasure belongs to the family of Giuki and has done so for at least two generations, as the Norse word 'arf' (= 'inheritance') implies, having presumably been amassed over the years by different rulers in that family.

The NL uses 'Nibelung' as a personal and a dynastic name but in the latter sense applies it to two distinct groups of people. In the first part of the epic it refers to King Nibelung of Nibelungland, whose sons, Kings Schilbung and Nibelung, are slain by Siegfried when he takes over their treasure.[14] Later, when Siegfried visits Nibelungland, it denotes the inhabitants of the country or at least the warriors.

In the second half of the poem, which begins with the Burgundians setting out for Etzel's land, 'Nibelungs' becomes a name for them, *i.e.* for Gunther's people, *who are now in possession of the treasure.* In the Ths. the land ruled by Gunnar is 'Niflungenland' and the people are 'Niflungs'.

The frequently-made assertion of a purely mythical origin of the 'Nibelung' name is, in contrast to the historical, untenable from a mythical-etymological standpoint. In the first place, the word itself does not occur in any mythological context in the literature, but only in relation to the Burgundians. From Snorri's *Edda*– but nowhere in the extant *Edda* poems – we have the place-name Niflheim.

Before the world began there existed only Ginnungagap, the Yawning Gulf, which was comprised of two contrasting regions: Muspellheim, full of flame and heat, and Niflheim, out of which 'cold and all terrible things blow up' (Snorri). Niflheim was uninhabited until Allfather cast the goddess Hel into it; he gave Hel the rule of nine worlds to which those people are sent who die on the sick bed or of old age. Thus the literal meaning of 'Niflung' or 'Nibelung', a native of Niflheim, has no application in a mythological context because no beings originate in Niflheim, they are only sent there after death. As Mone has observed:

> The root *niv* or *nov* expresses the damp location of a place. The Teutons make Nebel out of it, perhaps at first from the observation that fogs are more frequent at such places, but later they attached mythical concepts to the name that were quite foreign to it. Nevertheless these later notions became the prevailing popular view and very much obscured the simple origin. [15]

Furthermore, in view of the fact that a treasure accompanied suzerainty over a realm in the time of the Migrations, then logically the treasure belonged to someone who bore the family name of the royal dynasty; thus *not only the derivation of the name 'Nibelung' itself, but also the idea of an inherent connection in the NL between the bearers of the name Nibelung and the owners of the treasure, finds support in history.*

The nationalistic movement in nineteenth-century Germany awakened considerable interest in the ancient Germanic heritage of myth, legend and literature; scholars strove to analyse this rich body of culture and to discover its origins in the remote Germanic past. Their studies of the Nibelung saga show their awareness of the treasure's significance as a power-symbol and of an inherent association between the treasure and the people or peoples bearing the name of Nibelung. While keeping in mind the historical roots of these phenomena they attempted as well to construct elaborate mythical interpretations around the saga of the Nibelungs and their treasure, attempts which occasionally produced quite curious, even rather far-fetched results.

Karl Lachmann, in *Zu den Nibelungen und zur Klage: Anmerkungen*[16] whose inspiration for *The Ring* Wagner valued so highly, devotes much space to discussing the historical origin of the Nibelung name among the Rhenish Franks, while Göttling,[17] whose work had a decisive influence on Wagner in his perception of the identity between the Nibelung and the Barbarossa legends, attempts to trace a derivation of 'Nibelung' back to the Merovingian period and to establish the equation of 'Nibelung' with 'Gibeline' and 'Waiblingen' (home of Friedrich I), the latter with the aid of some specious etymological arguments which Wagner was later to digest and adapt in his important essay *Die Wibelungen: Weltgeschichte aus der Sage* (1848). Further, Göttling refers to a saga held by Swabian farmers that Attila, during his retreat from Gaul after the battle on the Catalaunian Plains, destroyed Burg Waiblingen which then had to be rebuilt; the common feature of destruction by the Huns shared by Gundahari's Burgundians and the family of Waiblingen Göttling adduces as indication of a closer and still earlier association between Nibelungs and Gibelines.

This historically-derived etymology of 'Nibelung' did not suffice for the nineteenth-century Germanists, however; wanting to establish the origins of this, in German culture, important name in the truly remote Germanic past they sought a mythical association as well, and it is upon this supposed dual origin, historical and mythical, of the name that the mythical interpretation of the Nibelung saga as a whole is based. For the 'mythical' etymology the name was associated with 'Niflheim' and 'Niflhel' of Nordic mythology. Lachmann first intimated the connection, postulating that 'Niflungar' means 'Nebelkinder', children of darkness or denizens of Niflheim/ Niflhel, and Grimm[18] then elaborated upon the concept, constructing theoretical early mythical histories of the mythical Nibelungs or Niflungs.

It was Lachmann who first identified these shadowy creatures of the night with the historically-derived Nibelungs:

> If we note that in Nordic mythology Nifelheim and Nifelhel are the names given to the cold part of the earth and the dwelling-place of the dead; if, moreover, we note that, while the Nordic saga first features dwarfs as rulers of the hoard, the South German legend, not without confusion, also makes out the first lords of the treasure (aside from Gunther and his entourage) to

be other Nibelungs, some of whom Siegfried slays, then it will be
difficult to doubt that both the former and the latter are of one
race, and this race is a supernatural one from the cold and misty
realm of the dead, to them the treasure belongs and to them it
returns. [19]

From this follows a mythological interpretation of the Siegfried
legend in which the hero is equated with a brilliant god of
peace:

> . . . The fable no longer depicts a hero but actually a brilliantly
> shining god, a god of peace through victory, who succeeds, not
> without punishment, in murdering the mysterious watchmen in
> the cold northern realm of the dead and seizing from the dragon
> the gold of the gods of the night. To be sure, through that
> robbery he wins wealth and wonderful powers, but he also falls
> under the spell of the demons. He must become their blood-
> brother, marry their sister, brave the flames with the demonic
> tool to win the radiant Valkyrie for the King of the realm of mist,
> overcome her resistance disguised as the King: with the ring
> from the treasure he marries her, but she becomes not his bride
> but the bride of his master; he is dead, stabbed by the fatal thorn,
> the son of horror, and the robbed gold is sunk into the Rhine. [20]

Wagner, who familiarised himself with many of these works,
derived much inspiration from their lines of thought – his essay
*Die Wibelungen* demonstrates the process by which he sought
to assimilate the material for his own purposes – yet he never
lost sight of the essential truths of the origins of the saga and the
hoard; he succeeded in adapting the various ideas to fashion a
dramatic structure that expresses the combined essence of the
mythical and historico-legendary meanings of the saga.

Wagner's awareness of the equation of the hoard with power
was manifest even before he came to write down a word of
dramatic text: his *Wibelungen* essay reveals his thoughts on the
subject in the early stages of their formation. The hoard had
already come to represent limitless power in what Wagner
considered to be the early, purely mythical forms of the
Nibelung legend, but above and beyond that he recognised
that the concept also had historical precedents in the treasure
of the royal Frankish dynasties and that it became still more
firmly established with each new victory achieved by the

Franks; such victories would have been, for example, those over the Romans, in which the Franks must have taken their opponents' war funds and imperial standards as booty (in this connection it is irresistible to wonder how much Wagner knew of Arminius). We shall see that Wagner's consciousness of these historical roots also had vital bearing on his view of the implications of the Nibelung name and the Nibelung 'race'.

Wagner believed that, in its most primitive version, what eventually developed into the Nibelung saga was a myth in which the proto-Siegfried appeared as a sun-god. In the earliest 'historical' manifestation of the legend Siegfried is recognisable as the hero who wins the Nibelung hoard and the unlimited power it brings. This hoard and the power

> remain the nucleus to which all further versions of the saga relate as its fixed central point: all striving and all struggling is for this hoard as the embodiment of all earthly power, and whoever possesses it, whoever rules through it, is or becomes a Nibelung. [21]

This last point is vital: not only is the hoard itself the unifying feature of the saga, but the name 'Nibelung' too runs through it like a red thread, borne by each of the hoard's possessors in turn; further, because the Nibelung name appears in what Wagner saw as both the 'mythical' and the 'historical' versions of the legend, it identifies the 'mythical' with the 'historical' Nibelungs, the former being, according to Wagner who follows Grimm and Lachmann, the 'Niflungar' or inhabitants of Niflheim, dwelling-place of the night-spirits, who are equated with the *Schwarzalben* or black elves, of whom Alberich is one: 'and this name [is found] again in the Frankish saga',[22] borne by those figures whose historical models possessed the royal blood of the Frankish kings, beginning with (or before) the Merovingians and continuing right through to the successors of Charlemagne. This concept –

> the, if not genealogical, then certainly mythological identity of the Frankish royal dynasty with the Nibelungs of the saga which in its later, more historical formation has taken over unmistakable features from the history of this clan and whose

central point still remains the possession of that hoard, the embodiment of ruling power [23]

– was to prove most essential to the dramatic structure of *The Ring* as noted at the beginning of this chapter. Of immeasurable value along with this was Lachmann's mythically-couched interpretation of the legend, with its identification of the people from whom Siegfried won the treasure with those who slew him to win it (back) from him and its reference to the thorn with which the hero is stabbed, which unmistakably recalls Balder and the mistletoe. In the light of this inspiration Wagner perceived the Nibelung saga *existing with equal validity on two levels, the mythical and the historico-legendary.* Essential on both levels, and in all versions from the most primitive of the myths to the expansive saga infused with historico-political overtones, is the balance, the *symmetry imparted by the hoard's being won back from the hero by those from whom he had won it.* In *myth*, as light (the sun-god) conquers dark, so does Siegfried kill the dragon and win the hoard. 'This is also the reason for his death,' observes Wagner, 'for the dragon's heir strives to win it back.'[24] That this feature continued in the further evolution of the Nibelung legend Wagner attributed to an incident supposedly from the annals of history. When dying, the early Frankish king, Chlodio, entrusted his three young sons to the protection of Merovech (Meroveus, eponymous founder of the Merovingian dynasty) who, however, seized the royal power for himself and banished the young boys. One of the sons was spared, and from his descendants rose the mighty Pippin family, who eventually 'completely deposed the drastically degenerated, power-ruined Merovingian clan'[25] and from whom Charlemagne arose to rule the entire German world. That there is no truth to this story, the ultimate source of which is undoubtedly some work written to denigrate the Merovingians and justify the Pippins' or Carolingians' seizure of the royal power of the Franks,[26] is irrelevant: what does matter is that Wagner, having read it, believed it, and regarded it as an *important influential factor in the symmetry of the legend in the hoard's having been seized and then regained by members of the original possessor's family:* the Burgundians who slay Siegfried for his treasure being, 'if not genealogically, then mythologically' of 'the same race' as the Nibelungs from whom he originally won it.

So far our main concern has been to examine the development of the *Ring Cycle* through tracing individual features back to their origins in history, legend and myth. But it is also possible to view its evolution *as an entity* from a source which is also considered as an entity, and the key to this is the concept, formulated by Wagner in his *Wibelungen* essay, of the Nibelung legend's evolution from, and appearance in, different forms on different levels of myth and legend, with the symmetrical ABA structure which represents, for example, night-day-night or a treasure's movement away from and back to its original owners, more or less discernible on each level. The Balder myth is one of the many forms the heroic story has taken: it must have been Lachmann's interpretation of the legend that brought home to Wagner the realisation that the mention of Balder as a separate figure from Siegfried would have been superfluous.

Theoretically Wagner could have dramatised his *Ring* all on any *one* of the levels: he could have chosen, for example, to portray a sun- or light-god who slays the dragon of the night and wins his treasure, and in turn is slain by the dragon's relatives; or he could have fashioned a more historically-entrenched hero such as the NL Siegfried, who conquers the Nibelungs and seizes their treasure, only later to be murdered for it by the Burgundians. Instead Wagner took an extraordinary course: *he chose to begin on the mythical and, in the middle of the drama, pass to the historico-legendary plane.* This was in keeping with the philosophical message with which he himself imbued the material, namely that the gods, represented by Wotan their leader, have got themselves into a situation in which they are powerless to act and must therefore relinquish the stage to the humans in hopes that the latter will succeed in putting things right.

Thus the *Ring Cycle* begins on the level of myth, in the realm of darkness inhabited by the Nibelung dwarfs. The leader of this 'army of the night' is Alberich, who becomes owner of the ring. That Siegfried wrests the ring and hoard not directly from Alberich but from Fafner does not constitute a contradiction of or departure from the essential myth, for in the first place it is consistent with Lachmann's reference to the hero's seizure *from the dragon* of the gold of the gods of the night, and moreover Fafner, who in his stupidity does not make use of the ring or hoard, can be considered rather a 'guardian' than an owner of the treasure, just as the dragon in Lachmann's re-telling guards the gold for the demons of the night. Siegfried's conquest of Fafner represents the point of unity between the hero's 'mythical' and 'historical' predecessors, from the brilliant, primitive sun-god to the shining Balder and the victorious Arminius, the pivot point which expresses the essence of their heroism and at which the drama is transposed from the mythical to the historico-legendary plane. Now the 'dragon's heir', the Nibelung who strives to regain the ring from the hero, will not be a mythical dwarf or dragon but the historico-legendary Hagen and his half-siblings, the Gibichungs.

Thus far we have seen important meeting points between myth and legend in *The Ring* to be Siegfried's absorption of Balder, Hagen's partial absorption of Loki and his 'reincarnation' of Loge. Now a further such point is Hagen and the Gibichungs' identification with the Nibelung dwarfs of *Das Rheingold* in that, in the context of the Siegfried myth-legend as understood by Wagner and the nineteenth-century German philologists, they embody in legendary terms what the Nibelung dwarfs embody in mythical terms: the race who lost the treasure to the hero and who then seek to regain it. In Hagen's case the identification is obvious for, as son of Alberich and half-brother of Gunther and Gutrune, he is literally 'of the same race' as both the Nibelungs and the

Gibichungs. But to understand how Wagner's Gibichungs too are 'of the same race' as the Nibelung dwarfs, although not in the genealogical sense, we must examine them more closely in terms of their literary models.

The Gibichungs of *The Ring* must have had an illustrious past, to judge from Brünnhilde's scathing remark to Gunther in *Götterdämmerung* Act II –

> Deep has sunk your glorious race
> to have borne such a coward as you

– derived from the NL in which Siegfried, as he lies dying, says, 'May God have mercy on me for ever having got a son who in years to come will suffer the reproach that his kinsmen were murderers.'[27] The sources vary with respect to how they name Gunther's family, whose historical predecessors are named in the *Lex Burgundionum* as Gibica and his sons Gundaharius, Gislaharius and Gundomaris. In the pure Nordic tradition the father of Gunnar and his siblings is called Giuki, the regular Norse equivalent of Gibich, and the term 'Giukungs' appears in *Skamma* while *Brot* refers to 'Giuki's house' in the sense of 'dynasty'. The Ths., on the other hand, breaks with tradition by calling Gunnar's father Aldrian. In the extant German sources only *Waltharius*, which does not directly concern the Siegfried or Nibelung legends, knows Gibich as Gunther's father: the NL inexplicably goes against tradition by calling the *paterfamilias* Dancrat, with King Gibich appearing not as a Burgundian king or even a relative of Gunther but as one of many royal vassals of Etzel who ride out with their men to greet Kriemhild upon her arrival in Hunland.

Therefore Wagner's specific use of the German appellation 'Gibichung' as a dynastic family name in the context of the Siegfried legend is an innovation, at least insofar as the practice does not survive in any extant source. Why did he adopt this term, allowing Gunther, Gutrune and their home (the Gibichung Hall) to be repeatedly referred to during *Götterdämmerung* by the name of a father who neither appears in nor has any bearing on the course of the drama? For enlightenment we must turn to Göttling, the scholar whose studies bore such fruit for Wagner, for it is he who, in the context of trying to prove the identity of Nibelungs and Gibelines, mentions the term Gibichung or 'Gibeching (= Giukung)' and the castle Gibichenstein near Halle in connection with the Gibeline family, and attempts to *equate Gibeching with Gibeline* and thus, by extension, *with Nibelung*. Therefore, in terms of Wagner's own historical-philological views the identification between his Nibelung dwarfs and his Gibichungs is an etymological one: *it is the name which underlines their 'racial' identity with the mythical Nibelung dwarfs of* Das Rheingold. Since the drama has passed from the mythical to the historico-legendary plane it was fitting that the people who seek to acquire Siegfried's ring bear what Wagner saw as the purely historico-legendary version of the 'Nibelung' name, which latter he believed had dual (mythical and historical) origin and which he therefore applies to his dwarfs with whom he saw the Gibichungs sharing racial identity. In view of this racial identity, then, we can perceive the Gibichungs not merely as Hagen's pawns in his plot against Siegfried but, more importantly, *as an essential factor in the symmetry of Wagner's drama*, those who lost the ring at the outset of the tetralogy now reappearing in a different guise to reclaim it from the hero. Yet the ultimate element of symmetry in the *Ring Cycle* is the ring itself, fashioned from the Rhine gold, which at the beginning of *Das Rheingold* glimmers in the depths of the Rhine and at the end of *Götterdämmerung* is returned there to its rightful place, and which, in between, runs its inexorable course as the object of 'all striving and all struggling . . . as the embodiment of all earthly power'; [28] indeed, without man's immemorial struggle for wealth and power there would be no 'history' and therefore no heroic legends.

## Notes

1. This subject has been exhaustively and admirably dealt with by Deryck Cooke in *I Saw the World End*.

2. Jung, p. 186.

3. This treasure is now in the Spanish National Museum, Madrid.

4. Gundahari has been thought of by some historians as an over-presumptuous young king who overestimated the power of his tribe.

5. *Cf.* NL and Ths.

6. Mone, p. 29.

7. The *-linc* or *-ling* form still exists in West Flanders.

8. Georg Holz, *Der Sagenkreis der Nibelungen*, quoted in Berndt, p. 69.

9. Mone, pp. 28f.; *cf.* also Berndt, pp. 112ff.

10. *Cf.* Deryck Cooke, pp. 93 and 196f.

11. Genzmer, p. 28.

12. Norse *arf*, which = 'inheritance'.

13. Norse *arfi Niflunga*, 'Nibelung inheritance'.

14. p. 27.

15. p. 29.

16. Berlin, 1836.

17. *op.cit.*

18. Jacob Grimm, *Deutsche Mythologie*.

19. p. 342.

20. p. 345.

21. *Die Wibelungen*: section 'Die Nibelungen'.

22. *ibid.*

23. *ibid.*

24. *ibid.*

25. *ibid.*

26. I have thus far been unable to trace the original, or Wagner's, source for this story.

27. p. 132.

28. *Die Wibelungen.*

# 8

# Conclusion

The importance of the role which history played in the fashioning of Wagner's *Ring* has generally been grossly underestimated. When Wagner first conceived the idea of a great heroic work he started from a historical standpoint, contemplating the Barbarossa and the Siegfried themes at the same time. When his reading of Göttling's *Nibelungen und Gibelinen* revealed to him the essential similarity between these two themes he discarded the Barbarossa in favour of the Siegfried idea; that is to say, he dropped the subject which was more firmly based in history in preference to that which possessed more mythical overtones.

But is one therefore justified in claiming that at this point Wagner's interest in history yielded to an interest in myth? Rather, it would be more accurate to say that the focus of his interest passed from the depiction of *specific heroes* in their historical context to the depiction of *types*, a process more akin to myth. Such a statement does not deny the fact that Wagner was ever aware of the interaction between history and myth in the formation of his source material – the poems, epics and sagas – and, moreover, that this awareness has influenced the moulding of the text of *The Ring*.

Therefore if history cannot, as stated at the outset, provide a new *interpretation* of *The Ring*, it can certainly help to clarify the *origin and inspiration* of certain elements in it. Examples of such elements have abounded throughout the foregoing study: the transition from the mythical to the historico-legendary level in the midst of the Cycle, which owes its complete naturalness and smoothness to Wagner's view that the Nibelung saga originated in myth and attained its further, most substantial development from events in Frankish history; the cowardly Gunther, disgrace of his 'glorious race', spiritually and perhaps physically related to the 'drastically degenerated, power-ruined clan' of the later Merovingians; the fact of the cataclysmic events' following upon Gunther's death and the destruction of the Gibichung Hall, which finds its embryonic form in the Burgundian holocaust but even more in the equation of the extinction of a dynasty – the destruction of the 'Gibelines' and their power – with the establishment of a new world order.

Concerning Wagner's use of mythology in *The Ring* Deryck Cooke remarks upon 'Wagner's total absorption in the mythology and his ability to contribute entirely original ideas to it, which carry complete conviction as being a natural part of it' (p. 335). The same is true regarding his incorporation of historical features into *The Ring*: the true significance of Wagner's awareness of the history-myth-legend interaction lies in the masterful and consistent way in which he wove all these elements into the variegated tapestry of characters and situations that comprise the plot, and especially in the perfect blending of his own 'original' historical elements – the best example of which is the father-betrayal theme represented by Hagen-Alberich, drawn not from pre-existing literary sources but directly from Frankish history as recounted by Gregory – with the rest. It is a testimony to the depth to which Wagner's mind was attuned to the spirit of the era in which these events occurred, that turbulent atmosphere of strife and struggle which passed from history to the treasury of literature which it inspired, and which in turn inspired Wagner to create a work which, while firmly anchored in flesh-and-blood figures from history, enshrines the timeless truths of myth.

# Bibliography

## Wagner's writings

*Richard Wagner: Die Musikdramen.* With forward by Joachim Kaiser. Hamburg, 1971.

*Skizzen und Entwürfe zur Ring-Dichtung,* ed. Otto Stroebel. Munich, 1930.

*Die Hauptschriften,* ed. Ernst Bücken. Stuttgart, 1956. 'Der Nibelungenmythus als Entwurf zu einem Drama,' pp. 92-103; 'Epilogischer Bericht über die Umstände und Schicksale, welche die Ausführung des Bühnenfestspiels "Der Ring des Nibelungen" bis zur Veröffentlichung der Dichtung desselben begleiteten,' pp. 302-314.

*Die Wibelungen: Weltgeschichte aus der Sage.* Leipzig, n.d.


## Original literary sources

*Die Lieder des Codex Regius nebst verwandten Denkmälern.* (Original language.) Gustav Neckel, ed.; 4th ed. by Hans Kuhn. Heidelberg, 1962.

*Die Edda,* transl. into German by Felix Genzmer. Düsseldorf/ Cologne, 1964.

*Den poetiska Eddan,* transl. into Swedish by Björn Collinder. 3rd ed., Forum Pocket, 1972. (This translation also contains extensive sections from the VS which fill in the lacunae between poems.)

*Valda sånger ur den poetiska Eddan,* transl. into Swedish by Karl Ljungstedt. Stockholm, 1904.

*Snorres Edda,* transl. into Swedish by Björn Collinder. Forum Pocket, 1970.

*Volsunga Saga,* transl. by William Morris with introduction by Robert W. Gutman. New York, 1962; 3rd ed., 1971.

*The Nibelungenlied,* transl. by A.T. Hatto. Penguin Classics, 1965; rev. ed., 1969.

## Other works

Berndt, Helmut. *Das 40. Abenteuer: Auf den Spuren der Nibelungen.* Munich, 1974.

Branston, Brian. *Gods of the North.* New York, 1980.

Campbell, Joseph. *The Masks of God: Creative Mythology.* London, 1974.

Cooke, Deryck. *I Saw the World End. A Study of Wagner's Ring.* London, 1979.

Davidson, H.R. Ellis. *Gods and Myths of Northern Europe.* Penguin Books, 1968.

Döbler, Hannsferdinand. *Die Germanen. Legende und Wirklichkeit von A-Z.* Prisma Verlag, 1975.

Donington, Robert. *Wagner's 'Ring' and Its Symbols.* London, 1963.

*Encyclopedia of World Mythology.* With foreword by Rex Warner. London, 1970-71, 1975.

Frauer, Ludwig. *Die Walkyrien der skandinavisch-germanischen Götter- und Heldensage.* Weimar, 1846.

Gibbon, Edward. *The Decline and Fall of the Roman Empire.* Abridged and with an introduction by Frank C. Bourne. New York, 1963.

Göttling, Karl Wilhelm. *Nibelungen und Gibelinen.* Rudolfstadt, 1816.

Gregory of Tours. *History of the Franks,* transl. by Lewis Thorpe. Penguin Classics, 1974.

Grimm, Jacob. *Deutsche Mythologie.* Göttingen, 1854.

Hallberg, Peter. *Den fornisländska poesin.* Verdandis Skriftserie 20. 2nd ed., Stockholm, 1962.

Jung, Ernst F. *Sie bezwangen Rom.* Düsseldorf and Vienna, 1976.

Koestler, Arthur. *The Thirteenth Tribe.* London, 1976.

Lachmann, Karl. *Zu den Nibelungen und zur Klage: Anmerkungen.* Berlin, 1836.

Lasko, Peter. *The Kingdom of the Franks.* London, 1971.

Loebell, Joh. Wilhelm. *Gregor von Tours und seine Zeit vornehmlich aus seinen Werken geschildert.* Leipzig, 1839.

Midderhoff, Hanns. 'Zur Verbindung der Nibelungenstoffe in der Edda,' *Zeitschrift für deutsches Altertum,* XCV, 4.

Mone, Franz Joseph. *Untersuchungen zur Geschichte der teutschen Heldensage.* Vol. 1 of *Bibliothek der gesammten deutschen National-Literatur von der ältesten bis auf die neuere Zeit,* Part II. Quedlinburg and Leipzig, 1836.

Müller, Wilhelm. *Versuch einer mythologischer Erklärung der Nibelungensage.* Berlin, 1841.

Nack, Emil. *Germanien.* Vienna and Heidelberg, 1958, 1977.

Ohlmarks, Åke. *Fornnordisk ordbok.* Kristianstad, 1975.

Riehl, Hans. *Die Völkerwanderung.* Pfaffenhofen/Ilm, 1976.

Tacitus. *Annalen,* transl. into German by Carl Hoffmann. Munich, 1978.

--------- *The Agricola and the Germania,* transl. by H. Mattingly, rev. by S.A. Handford. Penguin Classics, 1970.

Wallace-Hadrill, J.M. *The Barbarian West 400-1000.* Rev. ed., London, 1966.

-------- *The Long-haired Kings and Other Studies in Frankish History.* London, 1962.

Wapnewski, Peter. *Der traurige Gott. Richard Wagner in seinen Helden.* Munich, 1978.

Wisniewski, Roswitha. *Die Darstellung des Niflungenunterganges in der Thidrekssaga.* Tübingen, 1961.

# Index